SYNERGY

SYNERGY

Essentials of Scientific Research Writing

Editing Consultant: Katie Lloyd
A special thanks for Professor Hyonjin Kim for his support during the writing process
College English Program, Faculty of Liberal Education, Seoul National University

Seoul National University Press
1 Gwanak-ro, Gwanak-gu, Seoul 08826, Republic of Korea

Tel: +82-2-880-5252
Fax: +82-2-889-0785
E-mail: snubook@snu.ac.kr
Homepage: http://www.snupress.com

First Printing: March 20, 2020
ISBN 978-89-521-2884-3 03740

SYNERGY

Essentials of Scientific Research Writing

Nick Clements

Dylan G. Williams

Yoonsook Mo

Joel Park

SNUPRESS
Seoul National University Press

TABLE OF CONTENTS

Unit 2 The Scientific Research Paper

PREFACE

Introduction to the Textbook

Prospective Students

This book is aimed at intermediate-level non-native English speakers who are studying in an English for Academic Purposes (EAP) program. As the genre focus of this book entails scientific writing, it is naturally intended for students whose primary field of study is science or engineering. However, students in the social sciences can find value in this book as well due to the overlap in rhetorical structure, style, and research methods among these disciplines. The content focus of this book draws examples from science, engineering, and the social sciences; it does not exclusively focus on any single area.

The book is structured to guide students from basic writing principles at the sentence and paragraph level to ultimately authoring a complete scientific research paper. While this book does not provide specific advice on how to publish a scientific article, it will give anyone who uses it the necessary skills to write a scientific paper that is highly professional in both quality and appearance. As just one example of the latter, students who use this book will gain experience in the American Psychological Association (APA) style, a widely used writing style in both science and social science. Finally, because of the specific language that scientific writing demands, it can be of use for any students who want to hone their writing skills and express themselves with clarity, precision, and insight.

What Is Scientific Writing?

In science, the word 'synergy' denotes distinct elements which come together to produce a combined effect that is greater than the sum of its components. This concept certainly applies to the writing process of this book, which arose out of a long period of interaction and cooperation between the authors and resulted in the text that you are reading at this very moment. However, synergy applies to scientific writing as well. This is because it is a stepping-stone process that takes students from sentence-level writing, to paragraph structuring, to research paper section writing, to a complete research paper. All of the individual elements in the writing process are important, of course, but ultimately, it is the holistic impact of a piece of writing which makes the greatest impact on readers.

Synergy also represents the synthesis of your ideas as you are embarking upon a research project. This is an effect that can be brought about through collaboration as you discuss your ideas with both your instructor and classmates through a process of inquiry-based learning.

Finally, synergy is a concept that applies to scientific writing, which is delineated by its clear and straightforward prose style, adherence to systematic design and methodology, and analysis of data-driven results. As such, it is a special genre of writing that requires a specific understanding of its fundamental techniques and principles. This textbook will outline the key components and core skills required to write a scientific research paper. By the end of this textbook, students will have a solid understanding of the essentials of scientific research writing.

From Paragraph Writing to Research Paper Writing

This textbook is designed with a specific organizational approach which links paragraph writing with research paper writing. The paragraph represents an essential component in writing structure as it describes, explains, clarifies, and illustrates a single idea. All academic writing – and therefore all research paper writing – comprises a series of paragraphs. This is the basis for the two-unit structure of this textbook. Unit 1 consists of four paragraph chapters, and Unit 2 consists of six research paper chapters. Wherever possible, we have linked ideas from paragraph writing to a related idea in research paper writing.

Each chapter in this book generally contains a six-part structure which leads students through the process of understanding, individuating, analyzing, and writing. Paragraph chapters include a description section which explains the chapter's topic, a vocabulary section which contains key concepts, a purpose section which explains the main goal, a language section which contains key grammatical forms, a reading section which contains a paragraph model, and a writing section which requires students to apply all the ideas from the chapter. Research paper chapters (with a couple of minor exceptions in Chapter 5 and Chapter 8) include an overview section which summarizes the chapter's topic, a purpose section which explains the main goal, a language section which contains key grammatical forms, a goals and structure section which explains the key aims and basic organization, a reading section which contains one or more paragraph models, and a writing section which requires students to apply all the ideas from the chapter. As you become accustomed with the book, you will see that there are many shared structural elements between the paragraph and research paper chapters.

Lastly, the paragraph types that are covered in this textbook have been selected for a specific purpose, and are meant to develop key skills required in the research paper. The definition paragraph chapter develops skills for writing the introduction section of a research paper, as an author is usually required to define key terms and ideas in this section. The process paragraph chapter enhances skills for writing the methodology section of a research paper, as this section entails the description of all the procedural elements of the research project. The comparison/contrast paragraph chapter develops skills for writing the results section of a research paper, as this section often necessitates comparisons between groups of data.

In short, the structure of this book is rooted in making connections and unraveling patterns, one of the central aspects of academic and critical inquiry. What emerges from all of this, ideally, is synergy.

Unit 1

The Paragraph

1. Paragraph Fundamentals
2. The Definition Paragraph
3. The Process Paragraph
4. The Comparison/Contrast Paragraph

1 Paragraph Fundamentals

How to write a formal paragraph

Learning Outcomes:

- to think about the building blocks of writing
- to learn the functions of specific paragraph components
- to learn and practice different methods for creating the basic structure of a formal paragraph
- to learn and practice different sentence types such as complex, compound, and compound-complex sentences
- to analyze a formal paragraph and become familiar with the three paragraph types overviewed in this textbook
- to write a formal paragraph

1.1 Description

Formal writing can be described as a series of building blocks, with each block dependent on its previously established foundations. All writing systems begin with an alphabet; i.e. a system of individual letters. Letters can be combined to form words that convey distinct meaning and serve different grammatical functions; nouns describe objects, for example, while verbs describe actions. Words can then be combined to form sentences, which comprise at least a noun and a verb. Sentences, in turn, can be combined to form paragraphs: the central topic of this chapter.

Although a paragraph can be described as a group of sentences, this definition alone would ultimately be insufficient and incomplete. Like science, paragraphs need to have a basic structure and systematic approach.

1.1.A

With a partner, discuss how and why a paragraph is **not** just a group of sentences; in other words, add ideas to the initial definition. You might consider the first paragraph in this chapter as a way of exemplifying your explanation.

1.2 Vocabulary

The following are basic concepts that apply to paragraph writing:

concluding sentence	coherence	unity	topic sentence
supporting sentences	topic	transitions	controlling idea

1.2.A

Complete the sentences with one of the words in the box above.

1. The ____________ of a paragraph is its main subject.
2. The ____________ of a paragraph represents the specific viewpoint that the writer wants to express about the main subject.
3. The ____________ of a paragraph is a combination of the main subject of the paragraph and the writer's specific viewpoint about the main subject. It is usually located at the beginning of the paragraph.
4. Paragraphs must have strong ____________, which means that every sentence and idea relate to a single concept.
5. The ____________ of a paragraph give specific details and examples which strengthen the general idea of the paragraph.
6. A paragraph needs ____________ in order to create a strong flow and logical connection between sentences.
7. The ____________ of a paragraph refers to the way that all of the sentences and ideas fit together.
8. The ____________ of a paragraph is its last sentence.

1.3 Purpose

As suggested by the vocabulary exercise in 1.2.A, a paragraph can be defined as a collection of sentences that all share a common purpose. Because of this, we block these sentences together as a single entity. A single paragraph might be driven by a range of intentions — to inform, to persuade, or to entertain, for example — but all paragraphs should still contain the same structure and components.

The following four paragraphs provide an explanation for the vocabulary exercise in 1.2.A, as well as an overview of the essential components and organization scheme of a paragraph. First, a paragraph always begins with a single *topic* (1), which is the main subject of the sentence. However, a paragraph must have a distinct viewpoint as well; without a specific claim about the topic, a paragraph will feel vague and lack direction. We call this specific claim the *controlling idea* (2) of the topic. The *topic sentence* (3) of the paragraph, therefore, is a combination of the paragraph's topic and its controlling idea.

The topic sentence is the engine of the paragraph. It gives the writing purpose and direction, and helps the paragraph arrive at its intended destination. That single purpose establishes the *unity* (4) of the paragraph. The *supporting sentences* (5) provide specific examples of the general claim made by the topic sentence. They must relate to the topic sentence in a clear and direct manner. Supporting sentences can either express the distinct supporting ideas for the topic sentence or include concrete information such as facts, statistics, or quotations from credible sources. Any sentence that does not relate to the topic sentence weakens the paragraph's unity. Long ago, many people believed the world was flat, but that theory has been proven to be false. As you can see, the previous sentence clearly made no sense within the context of this entire paragraph; it is a good example of a statement that hinders the paragraph's unity.

A paragraph needs to include not only the basic components described above, but also *transitions* (6) which help to create a smooth flow and logical connections from one sentence and one idea to the next. Transitions might include expressions to include examples (such as 'for instance' or 'for example') logical connectors (such as 'hence' or 'consequently') sequence (such as 'to start' or 'next') or contrasting ideas (such as 'however' or 'on the other hand'). The effective use of transitions is one of many ways in which a writer can strengthen the *coherence* (7) of a paragraph, which relates to how all sentences and ideas ultimately fit together. A paragraph's coherence has a strong relationship with a larger aspect of writing that we call style, which can be roughly described as a writer's unique way of explaining his or her ideas. Writers with strong style typically have strong coherence and flow as well; these concepts are intrinsically connected.

All things must come to an end, of course, and the *concluding sentence* (8) represents the last statement in the paragraph. A good conclusion should aim for more than just repeating ideas that were already stated in the paragraph; it should also leave the reader with a final insight that arises naturally out of the text. This combination of both fulfilling the paragraph's unity and creating an original closing message is not easy to achieve but, when done well, is highly satisfying for both the reader and writer.

1.3.A

Read the paragraph below about the benefits of public transportation, then answer the discussion questions that follow in 1.3.B.

The Benefits of Public Transportation

Public transportation, a shared-ride mass transit system, can provide a number of benefits for a city and its community. First, public transportation can provide a relatively inexpensive system for helping a city's residents go back and forth between two distinct points. Because many people from low or lower middle-class income levels are unable to afford a car, they rely on buses, trains, or trolleys in order to get to and from work, as well as perform other routine tasks such as shopping at the grocery store or visiting the doctor. Secondly, public transportation is safer since bus drivers and train operators are skilled professionals who must follow strict policies set by the local government. As a result, taking public transportation leads to fewer accidents than driving an automobile. According to a study by the University of Central Florida, the intercity rail system is 20 times safer than driving, and the bus system is 60 times safer. A third important benefit is that it has been proven to reduce air pollution. A study by the state of Delaware, for instance, found that buses emit only 20% as much carbon monoxide as a single-driver automobile. In conclusion, the numerous advantages provided by public transportation make it an essential and socially responsible component of strong urban design, and no city can be considered complete without one.

1.3.B Discussion Questions

1. What is the topic of the paragraph? What is the controlling idea? What is the topic sentence?
2. Which supporting sentences in the paragraph's body contain the three main supporting ideas for the topic sentence?
3. Which supporting sentences include concrete information which exemplifies the three supporting ideas you discussed in the previous question?
4. What are some examples of transition expressions in the paragraph that strengthen its coherence?
5. What is the concluding sentence of the paragraph? What is the signal in this sentence that tells the reader that the paragraph is transitioning into its conclusion? Can you think of other signal expressions that are used with concluding statements?
6. What is the purpose of the concluding sentence? To give you a hint, concluding sentences usually contain one of three aims: (1) to summarize the main ideas of the paragraph (2) to make a prediction (3) to offer an opinion.

1.3.C

With a partner, consider the following topics as the basis for a paragraph: *energy*, *data*, and *disease*.

Brainstorm a controlling idea for each topic, then use this controlling idea to write a clear topic sentence that can guide an entire paragraph. The public transportation example from the paragraph in 1.3.A is provided as an example.

- **Topic**: *public transportation*
- **Controlling idea**: *can provide a number of benefits for a city and its community*
- **Topic sentence**: *Public transportation, a shared-ride mass transit system, can provide a number of benefits for a city and its community.*

- **Topic**: *energy*
- **Controlling idea**: ____________________
- **Topic sentence**: ____________________

____

- **Topic**: *data*
- **Controlling idea**: ______________________________
- **Topic sentence**: ______________________________

____

- **Topic**: *disease*
- **Controlling idea**: ______________________________
- **Topic sentence**: ______________________________

____

1.3.D

After writing the topic sentence, you then need to generate supporting details which specify the general claim of the topic sentence. One way to accomplish this is to ask simple questions, which is always a good starting point for developing ideas in both writing and science. Consider, for example, our topic sentence about public transportation:

- **Topic sentence**: Public transportation, a shared-ride mass transit system, can provide a number of benefits for a city and its community.

We might ask a range of questions in response to this claim. Each of them forces us to specify our ideas even further. Do keep in mind that we are still in the brainstorming phase of the writing process, so not all of our ideas will necessarily be used in our final paragraph.

1. *What* is the purpose of public transportation?
2. *What* are the particular benefits of public transportation?
3. *When* and *why* was public transportation first created?
4. *Who* benefits from public transportation?
5. *What* are the different types of public transportation?
6. *How* do cities decide *which* types of public transportation work best?

With a partner, pick one of the topic sentences that you wrote in the previous section, and write questions about your topic sentence that can help generate ideas for the supporting details of a paragraph.

1. ______________________________
2. ______________________________
3. ______________________________
4. ______________________________
5. ______________________________
6. ______________________________

1.3.E

We can now write supporting ideas for our paragraph in response to the questions that we wrote in the previous section.

- **Topic sentence**: Public transportation, a shared-ride mass transit system, can provide a number of benefits for a city and its community.

- **First supporting idea**: Public transportation can provide a relatively inexpensive system for helping a city's residents go back and forth between two distinct points.

- **Second supporting idea**: Public transportation is safer than driving. Bus and train operators are skilled professionals who must follow strict policies set by the local government and are much less likely to get into an accident.

- **Third supporting idea**: Public transportation can also reduce pollution since the smaller number of vehicles on the road leads to less carbon monoxide being emitted into the atmosphere.

With your partner(s), use the questions that you wrote in the previous section to generate three supporting ideas for your topic sentence.

- **Topic sentence**: ______________________________
  ____
  ____

■ **First supporting idea**: ____________________

____

____

■ **Second supporting idea**: ____________________

____

____

■ **Third supporting idea**: ____________________

____

____

1.4 Language

Thus far, we have remained at the sentence level with our writing exercises. In this section, you will learn about a number of concepts related to sentences that can strengthen the clarity, depth, and complexity of your writing style. These concepts include the following: (1) the *independent clause* (2) the *dependent clause* (3) the *compound sentence* (4) the *complex sentence* (5) the *compound-complex sentence*.

We will first turn our attention to the independent and dependent clause.

❖ Independent clause

An independent clause can be defined as a single idea that contains, at minimum, a subject and a verb. Independent clauses can vary enormously in their level of complexity. However, no matter how much or how little information the clause contains, it is still considered to be independent as long as it contains these two components. Ultimately, all independent clauses function as standalone sentences.

To further examine this idea, consider the following independent clause:

Example: *The human brain performs many crucial functions.*

The clause above includes a subject ('the human brain'), a verb ('performs'), and an object ('many crucial functions'). Although the clause is very simple, it is still independent — and therefore a standalone sentence — because it has a noun and a verb.

Let us now consider another independent clause which focuses on the same topic:

Example: *The human brain, which is the organ that regulates the central nervous system, performs many crucial functions.*

We can see that this clause clearly contains each component from the first example, while also including an adjective clause ('which is the organ that regulates the central nervous system'). The clause is more complex than the first example, but both are considered independent sentences.

We can continue to develop the complexity as much as we wish, as in the following example:

Example: *The human brain, the organ that regulates the central nervous system, performs many crucial functions and serves as the most vital element in the anatomical system.*

Again, despite the considerable variation in complexity between the three examples above, they are all ultimately the same in that they are independent clauses, and therefore standalone sentences.

❖ Dependent clause

A dependent clause is similar to an independent clause in that it contains a subject and a verb, but different in that it begins with a subordinator. Because it begins with a subordinator, a dependent clause cannot be considered a standalone sentence, and is therefore not independent. Consider the following dependent clause as an example:

Example: *Because the human brain performs many crucial functions*

Another name for a dependent clause is a *fragment*. It is called a fragment because it is incomplete; it needs more information in order to be considered an independent clause. Notice that the above example does not contain a period at the end because it cannot be considered a standalone sentence. Fragments are a very common type of error in student writing.

The subordinator of this clause is the word 'because'. The English language contains a range of subordinators that are commonly used in writing. The list below is a small subset.

Sample List of Subordinating Conjunctions

after	although	because	even though
if	since	that	unless
until	which	while	who

1.4.A Write independent and dependent clauses for the topics below.

1. Topic: *water*
   Clause type: *independent*

   ____
   ____
   ____

2. Topic: *vitamins*
   Clause type: *dependent*

   ____
   ____
   ____

3. Topic: *evolution*
   Clause type: *independent*

   ____
   ____
   ____

4. Topic: *artificial intelligence*
   Clause type: *dependent*

   ____
   ____
   ____

When separate individual clauses are combined together, they form what is called a compound sentence.

We will continue to use the topic of the human brain to consider the following example.

Example: *The skull protects the human brain. The spinal cord connects the brain to the central nervous system.*

While there is nothing wrong with the content or grammar of the two sentences above, the writing style still feels rather choppy and overly simplified. These two independent clauses could easily be combined to form a single compound sentence, as in the following:

Example: *The skull protects the human brain, and the spinal cord links the brain to the central nervous system.*

Now we can see the connection better; both the skull and the spinal cord are components of the skeletal system, which has an important relationship with the brain. Moreover, the writing feels smoother from the reader's perspective.

The example above is not the only way to form a compound sentence, though. Consider the following alternative:

Example: *The skull protects the human brain; furthermore, the spinal cord links the brain to the central nervous system.*

〉**Question:** What is the difference between the first and second compound sentence examples? Specifically, how do they differ in their linking word and their punctuation?

To answer the question above, there are two ways in which we can form a compound sentence in English. The first method uses a *coordinating conjunction*; the second uses a *conjunctive adverb*.

The coordinating conjunction of the first compound sentence example is the word 'and'. Notice that it is immediately preceded by a comma. There are a number of very common coordinating conjunctions in English, and each serves a different purpose. The punctuation is the same in each case, though; coordinating conjunctions are always preceded by a comma.

The **seven** primary **coordinating conjunctions** are as follows:

Coordinating Conjunction	Function	Example
for	to explain the reason	Solar power is being increasingly used in desert regions, **for** the sun is virtually always present in this type of landscape.
and	to add a related idea	Solar power is being increasingly emphasized in desert regions, **and** many countries in these areas are funding projects to move toward this alternative energy system.
nor	to add a related idea in the negative form	The government has demonstrated little interest in investing in solar power, **nor** has it explored other types of alternative energy sources.
but	to add an opposing idea	The southern region of the country has dedicated many resources toward converting to solar power, **but** the northern region has placed very little emphasis on this issue.
or	to add a possible idea/ consequence	The committee reported that the government needs to begin investing in solar power, **or** the country will eventually suffer serious consequences from overreliance on fossil fuels.
yet	to add an unexpected idea/consequence	More than 90% of the country is desert, **yet** little effort has been made to create solar power grids by the government.
so	to add a logical result	The sun is virtually always present in desert regions, **so** solar power is being increasingly used in these types of landscapes.

Notice that by taking the first letter of each coordinating conjunction (for, and, nor, but, or, yet, so), we can form the acronym FANBOYS. Remembering this acronym can help you better remember the coordinating conjunctions.

In the case of the coordinating adverb, a semicolon is used to connect the independent clauses instead of a comma. Consider the following chart of coordinating adverbs and their corresponding examples.

Coordinating Adverb	Function	Example
furthermore in addition moreover	to add a related idea	Solar power is being increasingly emphasized in desert regions; **moreover**, many countries in these areas are funding projects to move toward this alternative energy system.
however on the other hand in contrast	to add an opposing idea	The southern region of the country has dedicated many resources toward converting to solar power; **on the other hand**, the northern region has placed very little emphasis on this issue.
otherwise	to add a possible idea/consequence	The committee reported that the government needs to begin investing in solar power; **otherwise**, the country will eventually suffer serious consequences from overreliance on fossil fuels.
nevertheless nonetheless in spite of this	to add an unexpected idea/ consequence	More than 90% of the country is desert; **in spite of this**, very little effort has been made to create solar power grids by the government.
consequently hence therefore	to add a logical result	The sun is virtually always present in desert regions; **hence**, solar power is being increasingly used in these types of landscapes.
for example for instance	to provide an example	Solar power is being increasingly emphasized in desert regions; **for instance**, The United Arab Emirates has invested billions of dollars in an attempt to create the world's first carbon-free city.

1.4.B

Create compound sentences below by using the coordinating conjunctions in parentheses to add another independent clause. Make an appropriate modification to the punctuation if needed.

1. Most engineers recommend building this product out of steel. (for)

____

____

2. The ecosystem contains a diverse range of plants. (and)

____

____

3. None of the test subjects had any significant health issues. (nor)

4. The average rainfall last year declined by 5%. (but)

5. The automobile's electrical system needs to be modified. (or)

6. The average temperature last year increased by 2 ℃. (yet)

7. The chemical bond is considered to be highly unstable. (so)

1.4.C

Create compound sentences below by using the coordinating adverbs in parentheses to add another independent clause. Make an appropriate modification to the punctuation if needed.

1. Researchers discovered significant levels of radioactivity in the region. (furthermore)

2. The area's squirrel population has increased every year over the past decade. (however)

3. The engineers reported that the system needs to be upgraded very soon. (otherwise)

4. The country has virtually no natural resources. (nevertheless)

____

____

5. The country's landscape is primarily mountainous. (therefore)

____

____

6. Exercise has been proven to yield significant health benefits. (for instance)

____

____

7. Diet soda contains fewer calories than regular soda. (in spite of this)

____

____

Recall from 1.4.A our dependent clause example:

Example: *Because the human brain performs many crucial functions*

〉**Question:** How could we modify this fragment so that it is an independent, standalone sentence? Can you use information from the independent clause examples in 1.4 to accomplish this task?

The answer to the above question relates to the second type of sentence in this section: the complex sentence. A complex sentence is a combination of an independent clause and one (or more) dependent clause(s). Hence, all dependent clauses must be attached to an independent clause in order to function as standalone sentences. We might, then, use ideas from the last independent clause in 1.4 to create a complex sentence out of our dependent clause.

Example: *Because the human brain performs many crucial functions, it is fair to say that it is the most vital element in the anatomical system.*

Notice that a comma is used to separate the dependent from the independent clause in the example above. This is because the dependent clause *begins* the sentence. If the dependent clause *ends the sentence*, on the other hand, then no comma should be used, as in the following example:

Example: *It is fair to say that the human brain is the most vital element in the anatomical system since it performs many crucial functions.*

1.4.D

Create complex sentences below by completing the blanks. Use appropriate punctuation when necessary.

1. After the clinical drug trials have been completed ______________________________

   ____

2. Until Polish astronomer Nicolaus Copernicus provided clear evidence of a heliocentric universe ____

   ____

3. ______________________________________ although there is a very small probability that the temperature change was merely a random fluctuation.

4. ____ who is widely credited with inventing wireless technology.

1.4.E

Using the dependent and independent clauses that you developed in 1.4.A, write complex sentences for the same topic. If needed, you can use the sample list of coordinating conjunctions at the end of 1.4.A for help.

1. Topic: *water*

   ____

   ____

2. Topic: *vitamins*

   ____

   ____

3. Topic: *evolution*

   ____

   ____

4. Topic: *artificial intelligence*

____

____

Thus far, we have considered the compound sentence and the complex sentence. This leads to the third type of sentence for consideration: the compound-complex sentence. A compound-complex sentence is a combination of at least two independent clauses and (one or more) dependent clause(s). We can build upon our previous example of the human brain to illuminate this point.

Example: *Because the human brain performs many crucial functions, it is fair to say that it is the most vital element in the anatomical system; consequently, it will continue to exist at the forefront of medical research.*

1.4.F

Use two complex sentences from 1.4.E to create a compound-complex sentence.

1. ____

2. ____

1.5 Reading

1.5.A

Read the following paragraph about the human brain, then answer the discussion questions that follow.

The Human Brain

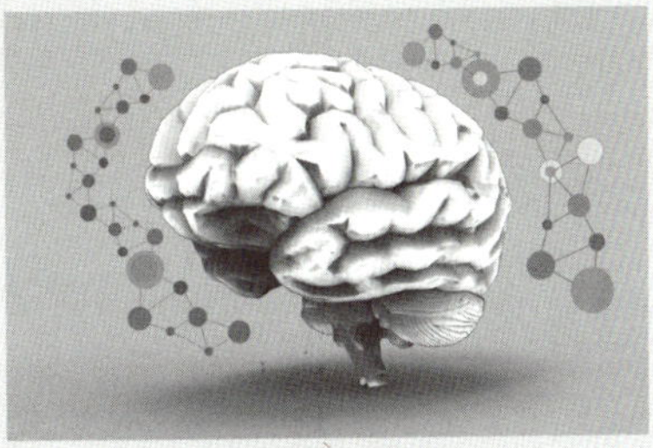

The human brain, the organ that controls the central nervous system, is organized by three primary regions which can be described by both their structure and function. Structure refers to the specific physical area where individual regions are located; function, on the other hand, refers to the set of tasks performed by the aforementioned three regions. The first is the cerebrum, which is located in the upper part of the brain. It is responsible for most of the brain's higher functions such as language, learning, and memory. The second region is called the cerebellum, which can be found in the brain's lower section. The cerebellum controls essential body functions such as balance, posture, and coordination. The third region, located in the center of the brain, is the limbic system. This region regulates basic bodily functions such as the perception of and response to hunger, thirst, or pain. In turn, each of the three regions includes subregions which perform very specific functions. For instance, the frontal lobe is one of the four lobes in the cerebrum; it controls creative thought, problem solving, intellect, judgment, behavior, attention, abstract thinking, and personality. A final point to note is that while the core structure and functions of the brain remain essentially the same throughout one's lifetime, it is not completely fixed. By learning new tasks, solving problems, and maintaining a healthy and active lifestyle, a person can increase the number of connections in his or her brain, which means that it is capable of evolving through experience. In short, although all humans are born with brains that share a similar structure and set of functions, there is still substantial room for choice and free will; the old saying that we are what we make of ourselves appears to actually have some scientific validity.

1.5.B Discussion Questions

1. What is the topic sentence of this paragraph? How does the topic sentence shape and guide the writing in the paragraph?
2. What are the essential supporting details for the topic sentence?
3. What are some examples of transitions in this paragraph which help to improve its coherence?
4. Find examples of any of the following: (1) dependent clause (2) independent clause (3) compound sentence (4) complex sentence (5) compound-complex sentence.
5. What is the purpose of the concluding sentence?

This textbook includes chapters on three specific types of paragraphs: definition, process, and comparison/contrast. The paragraph in 1.5.A best fits the model of a definition paragraph. It defines what the brain is, and explains its essential components and functions.

As was mentioned in the beginning of this chapter, a single topic can have a range of controlling ideas, which means that it could fit into a broad spectrum of paragraph types as well.

1.5.C

In this exercise, you are going to think about how to write a process and/or a comparison/contrast paragraph about the human brain. Consider the following two questions:

1. A process paragraph explains how something works. Do you know how the brain works? For example, how does the brain send a signal to move parts of the body such as the hands, arms, or legs? How does the brain store memories?

   What would your topic sentence be for such a paragraph? What would the supporting details be?

2. A comparison/contrast paragraph examines similarities and differences between two different people, objects, or ideas. What are the similarities and differences between the brain and another vital organ such as the heart? How are the brain and the heart similar, and how are they different?

   What would your topic sentence be for such a paragraph? What would the supporting details be?

1.6 Writing

1.6.A

You are now ready to write your own paragraph. Use ideas that you have discussed in this chapter to write a complete paragraph with its requisite topic sentence, supporting sentences, and concluding sentence. While writing, think about using transitions to improve the flow of your writing from one sentence and one idea to the next in order to help the reader follow your ideas better. Finally, think about writing beyond simple sentences in your writing; wherever possible, try to use compound, complex, and/or compound-complex sentences.

When you are finished, exchange your paragraph with a partner and offer appropriate feedback on his or her writing.

Revision Checklist

Did you ...

- ☐ create a topic sentence which clearly guides the entire paragraph?
- ☐ use supporting sentences to elaborate upon and provide concrete details for the general ideas of the topic sentence?
- ☐ make effective use of transitions between sentences and ideas?
- ☐ use a range of sentence types such as simple, compound, complex, and compound-complex?
- ☐ write a conclusion that ends the paragraph by leaving the reader with food for thought?

2 The Definition Paragraph

How to define concepts, objects, and their components

Learning Outcomes:

- to learn the key points of a definition
- to become familiar with assigning a category to a concept or object
- to understand the purpose of a definition paragraph
- to use adjective clauses and appositives
- to critique a definition paragraph
- to define and explain a concept or object with a formal academic style

2.1 Description

Scientific writing always needs to begin with a clear definition of ideas for the reader. This helps make the text unambiguous and straightforward in its intentions. In this chapter, we are going to examine some essential features of writing a definition, which entails a statement (or group of statements) that explains the meaning of a concept or object to make it clear for the audience. The key points that a definition should include are as follows:

- enable understanding of concepts or objects
- reduce ambiguity of concepts or objects
- provide concrete details about concepts or objects

2.1.A

What type of category would you assign a computer mouse?

____

____

What makes this object unique? What special features does it have?

____

____

2.2 Vocabulary

A good definition first entails classifying a term or object into a group which has similar characteristics. The group that a term or object belongs to is called the *category*.

2.2.A

Fill in the blanks with the most suitable category in the box.

technician	system	instrument	utensil	natural disaster
planet	disease	beverage	tool	social media application

1. A calculator is a/an ____________________.
2. Instagram is a/an ____________________.
3. Jupiter is a/an ____________________.
4. A computer specialist is a/an ____________________.
5. A spork is an eating ____________________.
6. An earthquake is a/an ____________________.
7. Parkinson's is a/an ____________________.
8. The subway is a transportation ____________________.
9. A voltmeter is a/an ____________________.
10. Sprite is a/an ____________________.

2.2.B

Fill in the blanks with an appropriate term or object not used in 2.2.A to match the category provided (use a/an when necessary).

1. ____________________ is a technician.
2. ____________________ is a transportation system.
3. ____________________ is an instrument.
4. ____________________ is an eating utensil.
5. ____________________ is a device.
6. ____________________ is a planet.

7. ______________________________ is a disease.
8. ______________________________ is a beverage.
9. ______________________________ is a natural disaster.
10. ______________________________ is a social media application.

2.3 Purpose

The purpose of a definition is not only to assign a category to a term or object, but also to provide information that makes it distinct within its own category and to outline characteristics which give the reader concrete details about the term or object.

As mentioned previously, we can categorize a computer mouse as a type of device, but what kind of device is it? What makes it different from other devices? Does this device have any special features? These types of questions are necessary to help provide information that gives the reader a better understanding of the term or topic and see what makes it different from other terms or objects in the same category.

Consider some of the following characteristics which make a computer mouse unique as a device:

- It connects to a computer.
- It makes it easy to use a computer.
- It allows the user to manipulate and interact with various programs and tasks.
- It is controlled by hand.
- It has an optical sensor.

We can see in the five points above a broad set of information about a computer mouse. In order to craft the information into formal writing, we need to strike an optimal balance. On the one hand, we need to include enough information into one sentence that vividly explains the term or topic to the reader; on the other hand, we should not overload the reader with too much information.

- A computer mouse connects to a computer and is controlled by hand to easily manipulate and interact with various programs and tasks.

> Notice that the optical sensor feature was not included since it would overload the reader with too much information

Now that we have collected all the requisite information for our definition, we can begin by presenting the term or object and assigning a category.

A computer mouse is a device.

We can then add the sentence we just created which contains all the unique information about the computer mouse to this sentence as follows:

A computer mouse is a device that connects to a computer and is controlled by hand to easily manipulate and interact with various programs and tasks.

2.3.A

For the terms or objects you chose from 2.2.B, write distinguishing features that make your terms or objects unique.

Example:

1. *An X-ray specialist is a technician.*
   - *uses cutting edge imaging machines*
   - *takes images of the body's internal anatomy*
   - *is not a medical doctor*

2. ______________________ is a transportation system.
   -
   -
   -

3. ______________________ is an instrument.
   -
   -
   -

4. ______________________________ is an eating utensil.
    -
    -
    -

5. ______________________________ is a device.
    -
    -
    -

6. ______________________________ is a planet.
    -
    -
    -

7. ______________________________ is a disease.
    -
    -
    -

8. ______________________________ is a beverage.
    -
    -
    -

9. ______________________________ is a natural disaster.
    -
    -
    -

10. ______________________________ is a smartphone application.
    -
    -
    -

2.4 Language

In this section, we are going to consider some grammatical forms that are commonly used in definition writing, beginning with the *adjective clause*. An adjective clause adds distinct features to a category after it has been assigned. An adjective clause is also known as a relative clause and is the part of a sentence that gives us more information about a particular term or object. Adjective clauses can be classified into two types: *defining adjective clauses* and *modifying adjective clauses*. The relative pronouns *which*, *who*, and *that* are used to make adjective clauses in sentences.

- *which* is used with things
- *who* is used with people
- *that* can replace which or who

A defining adjective clause (also known as an essential adjective clause) provides information that is necessary to define or identify a noun.

Examples: *The beaker <u>that has the red label</u> needs to be sterilized.*
The compass <u>which was dropped</u> requires maintenance.
The student <u>who was sick last class</u> will be absent today.

Grammar Point

"that" is used only for defining adjective clauses

If the adjective clauses were not present in each of the examples, it would be difficult or even impossible to know or identify exactly what the noun in each sentence was referencing. We would not know which beaker needs to be sterilized, which compass requires maintenance, or which student will be absent today.

A modifying adjective clause (also known as a non-essential adjective clause) provides extra information that is not necessary to define or identify the noun. Since this type of adjective clause adds extra non-essential information, commas are required to separate it. Notice that in the three examples below, we could delete the underlined adjective clause and still easily identify the noun.

Examples: *Professor Adams, who teaches Physics 101, will be retiring this year.*
Snowdon, which is Wales' highest mountain, is located in Gwynedd.
All science journal publications can be found in the Natural Sciences Library, which is located next to the central gymnasium.

Grammar Point

Only modifying adjective clauses require commas.
NOT defining adjective clauses.

2.4.A

Add distinguishing features to each sentence from 2.3.A using *which*, *who*, or *that*. You do not need to use all the information that you previously included.

1. **Example**: *An X-ray specialist is a technician who uses cutting edge imaging equipment to take images of the human body's internal anatomy.*
2. ______________________________
3. ______________________________
4. ______________________________
5. ______________________________
6. ______________________________
7. ______________________________
8. ______________________________
9. ______________________________
10. ______________________________

A full definition includes three parts: the term or object, category, and distinguishing features.

Term/Object	Category	Distinguishing Features
stapler	mechanical device	joins paper together with the insertion of a staple
compass	instrument	shows direction by using a diagram with cardinal points
carnivore	animal	survives by mainly eating meat or the flesh of animals

2.4.B

Write a sentence which describes the following terms or objects with a complete definition.

Example: *Stapler- A stapler is a mechanical device that combines paper together with the insertion of a staple.*

Bluetooth- ______________________________

____

Hovercraft- ______________________________

____

Tablet computer- ______________________________

____

Museum- ______________________________

____

Facebook- ______________________________

____

Diabetes- ______________________________

____

Appositives are the second grammatical form commonly used to modify a noun. They serve the same purpose as the adjective clause, but the language used to write them is slightly different. An appositive is also the part of a sentence used to give more information about a noun right beside it. However, an appositive uses a noun or noun phrase instead of an adjective clause. Like adjective clauses, appositives can be either essential or non-essential. Non-essential appositives are always bounded by commas, as in the examples below.

Example: *A prokaryote, a unicellular organism, is a cell without a nucleus.*

A product of Apple, the iPhone is considered to be the world's first smartphone.

Bibimbap, a Korean traditional dish of mixed rice and vegetables, is very popular with people visiting South Korea.

Grammar Point

Commas are needed before and after an appositive except when the appositive begins or ends a sentence. For an example, examine the iPhone sentence above.

2.4.C

Insert an appositive into the following sentences to provide additional information.

Example:

Aqua Regia can dissolve gold and platinum.

Aqua Regia, a very dangerous acid, can dissolve gold and platinum.

1. Namsan Tower is one of the most popular tourist attractions in South Korea.

2. A flu shot is given to protect people from getting sick.

3. A processor is essentially the engine of a computer.

4. The octopus is one of the most mysterious creatures in the animal kingdom.

____

____

5. The symptoms of bronchitis may include severe coughing and a sore throat.

____

____

2.5 Reading

2.5.A

Read the title of the following paragraph and think of what possible information may be provided about the topic. After brainstorming, read the entire paragraph about a computer mouse and consider the types of questions that the paragraph is answering.

Computer Mouse: Components and Functions

A computer mouse is a device that connects to a computer and is controlled by hand to easily manipulate and interact with various programs and tasks. The name originates from its similarity in shape to an actual mouse, particularly the tail. Most mouse devices comprise a left button, a right button, and a scroll wheel, which is used for easily moving up or down through pages. Initially, a mouse was physically connected to a computer using a cable, but many are now connected remotely. In addition, the mouse originally used a rubber ball, which was located underneath, to control the pointer on the computer screen. However, it has now been replaced by an optical sensor for more accuracy. For many people, it is difficult to imagine using a computer without a mouse as it helps them easily perform various tasks. For example, users can almost effortlessly shop on the Internet by clicking on the items they want or scrolling through the shop's website to see what is offered. Furthermore, computer gamers rely on a computer mouse to allow the user to navigate through various first-person shooter games, which are games played through the perspective of the game's character. Without a computer mouse, many of these popular games would be impossible to play since it is a crucial device to play the games properly. Although the technology of computers improves every day, the mouse will continue to be an essential device for using a computer effectively.

2.5.B

Identify what types of questions are being answered in this paragraph and explain why this information is helpful to the reader.

Example: *Why is it called a mouse?*

→ *This information can be helpful to the reader because it is unusual to have a device with a name of an animal.*

- ______________________
  → ______________________
- ______________________
  → ______________________
- ______________________
  → ______________________
- ______________________
  → ______________________
- ______________________
  → ______________________

2.5.C

Answer the following discussion questions about the mouse paragraph.

1. In the first sentence, what is the term or object, what is the category, and what are the distinguishing features used to make a complete definition?
2. How does this paragraph use an example to give information about a mouse?
3. What is the purpose of the last sentence?

2.6 Writing

The goal of a definition paragraph's topic sentence is simple and straightforward: to write a definition of the term or topic. The sentence structure for this definition should include the term or object, the category, and the distinct features as we previously learned. After the topic sentence, the writer then needs to add supporting sentences to provide more information so that the term or topic can be fully understood.

The supporting sentences should create a clear and comprehensive picture of the specific term or object you are trying to define through the use of examples, specific details, and descriptions.

In order to create a thorough set of supporting details, you should begin by answering questions such as:

- What does it look like?
- What does it do?
- What is it used for?
- What other types are there?

Example: Stapler

- *What does it do?*
  → *The primary function of a stapler is to combine sheets of paper together by driving a thin metal staple through them.*
- *What is it used for?*
  → *The purpose of a stapler is to hold sheets of paper together to easily keep them organized.*

2.6.A

Practice thinking of words to describe the objects in this exercise.

1. 
____
____
____
____

2. 
____
____
____
____

3. 
____
____
____
____

4. 
____
____
____
____

Think carefully about which questions are relevant to your topic and which answers are useful in delivering information to give the reader a full understanding of your term or topic.

2.6.B

Practice brainstorming for a definition paragraph.

Choose a term or object: ______________________________

Write a topic sentence: ______________________________

____

Create and answer questions about your topic that will help the audience understand your topic.

Example: *Who can use it?*
What does it do?

- ______________________________
  → ______________________________
- ______________________________
  → ______________________________
- ______________________________
  → ______________________________
- ______________________________
  → ______________________________
- ______________________________
  → ______________________________
- ______________________________
  → ______________________________
- ______________________________
  → ______________________________
- ______________________________
  → ______________________________
- ______________________________
  → ______________________________

2.6.C

What is a computer? Try to define a computer by using expressions that we have practiced and write questions which help generate information about a computer.

2.6.D

Try answering your questions from the previous exercise to gather information about a computer.

2.6.E

Now that you have your information, write a short definition paragraph of a computer.

〉**Note**: You do not have to include all the information; moreover, you can add your own information and organize your paragraph however you wish.

When you are finished, you can compare your paragraph with your partner(s) to examine similarities or differences.

Remember to include a topic sentence, supporting details, and a concluding sentence.

2.6.F Read the following sample paragraph.

What Is a Computer?

A computer, an electronic device that manipulates information, is a combination of various components and has a wide range of uses, functions, and types. To start with its components, computer consist of both hardware and software. Hardware comprises any physical parts of the computer, which includes all the internal components such as the motherboard and power supply; it also consists of the external parts such as the monitor and the keyboard. Software, on the other hand, is a set of instructions that tells the hardware what to do, such as a web browser, media player, or word processor. People use software programs for a variety of reasons: to write a paper, manage their money, watch movies, or video chat with friends who live halfway around the world. Computers can not only perform a variety of functions, but also consist of many types which depend on a person's needs. For example, personal computers include desktop computers, which are stationary, and laptop computers, which essentially have the same capabilities as a desktop computer, but in a more portable package. Moreover, computers come in many other shapes and sizes. Mobile phones, tablets, game consoles, and even TVs have built-in computers, although they may not do everything a desktop or laptop can do. In short, the size, shape, and capabilities of computers will continue to change and evolve in the future, but their basic framework will essentially remain the same.

2.6.G

Answer the following discussion questions about the computer paragraph.

1. Can you find examples of appositives and/or adjective clauses in this paragraph?
2. Can you find examples of transition signals or expressions in this paragraph? What is the specific purpose in each case?
3. What is the purpose of the concluding sentence?
4. Why is a semicolon used on the seventh line of the paragraph?
5. Why is a colon used on the tenth line of the paragraph?

Writing Your Definition Paragraph

- Now that you have completed Chapter 2, it is time to think about the definition paragraph that you will write for your assignment.
- You are free to choose any term or topic to write about that relates to engineering, science, or social science. Here are some example topics:
  - *Autonomous Vehicle*
  - *Crypto Currency*
- Prior to writing your definition paragraph, you should discuss your chosen topic with your instructor to ensure that it adequately meets the assignment requirements. You should also follow the specific formatting/evaluation criteria given to you by your instructor.
- Before you start drafting, you should go through the pre-writing process and create a clear outline that shows the supporting sentences which explain what your term or topic is.
- After you have created your rough draft, you should use the revision checklist below to make editorial changes.

Revision Checklist

Did you ...

☐ write a topic sentence which includes the term or object, category, and distinguishing features?

☐ use supporting sentences to describe specific details?

☐ provide information about your topic to make it more vivid for the reader?

☐ use an example as supporting information about your topic?

☐ use adjective clauses to give more information about nouns?

☐ use appositives to modify nouns?

☐ write a concluding sentence that provides additional insight into your term or object?

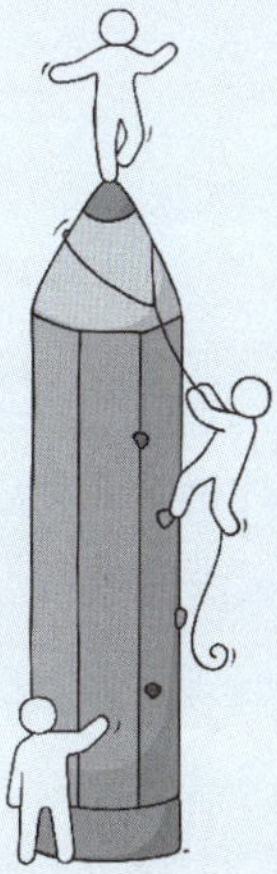

❸ The Process Paragraph

How to explain a procedure or method

Learning Outcomes:

- to describe a process
- to learn common verbs and sequencing expressions
- to understand the purpose of a process
- to use active/passive voice and cause-and-effect
- to critique a process paragraph
- to write about processes with an academic style

3.1 Description

The photo below is of the Coiling Dragon Cliff Skywalk, a glass-bottom bridge located on the side of Tianmen Mountain in Zhangjiajie National Forest Park, Hunan Province, China.

3.1.A

With your partner(s), brainstorm a minimum of 6 steps that were involved in the construction of this skywalk.

3.2 Vocabulary

The following are common verbs to use when describing processes in engineering, science, or social science disciplines:

measure	model	observe	sort
construct	test	predict	label

3.2.A

Complete the sentences with one of the verbs. In some cases, you may need to change the form of the verb.

1. First, sensors and cameras were used to ____________ the weather in the area and collect data about it.
2. During the design phase, the Skywalk was ____________ to visualize its form, structure, and appearance.
3. Before construction began, every component was ____________ to fit the exact specifications.
4. While building, it was important to accurately ____________ each section into the proper order.
5. Subsequently, everything was ____________ with a numbering system.
6. At this point, it was difficult to ____________ how long constructing the Skywalk would take.
7. The Skywalk was ____________ over a period of 6 months.
8. Lastly, when finished, the structure was rigorously ____________.

When describing processes in engineering, science, or social science disciplines, the following are a list of possible words/phrases to *communicate sequence*:

before long	as soon as	upon reflection	next
lastly	to begin with	in advance	in time

At which stage of a process would you use these *sequence expressions*?

3.2.B

In the *words/phrases* column, match the *sequence expressions* from above to the appropriate *stage* in a process.

STAGE	WORDS/PHRASES
1. before the beginning	
2. at the beginning	
3. to introduce a step	
4. after a short while	
5. after a longer period	
6. near simultaneous occurrences	
7. at the last step	
8. after the end	

3.2.C

Using the verbs from 3.2.A and the sequence expressions from 3.2.B, write eight sentences to describe the steps involved in a process of your choice.

Follow the given example.

Example: *It is important to precisely <u>measure</u> a wall <u>in advance</u> before putting up a shelf.*

1. ______
2. ______
3. ______
4. ______
5. ______
6. ______
7. ______
8. ______

3.3 Purpose

In scientific disciplines, the purpose of a process paragraph is to provide information.

e.g. providing an explanation of how something works, or providing knowledge and understanding of the stages involved in a process.

An *informational* process paragraph gives information (e.g. how a flower germinates). This provides the reader with knowledge and understanding of the stages involved.

Read the paragraph below which explains how to make a bouncy bubble.

The Optimal Method for Making a Bubble Bounce

To determine the optimal method for making a bouncy bubble, the following apparatuses were used: dish soap, a bubble wand (a straw-like pipe for blowing bubbles), a small cup, a cotton glove, and water. A number of stages were then conducted to discover the optimal way of getting the bubble to bounce. In the first stage, the solution was made from 3 parts water (150 ml) and 1 part dish soap (50 ml). Next, the actual experiment began. In the first part of the experiment, a bubble was blown to roughly the size of the circumference of a standard cup. After that, the flat palm of the researcher's upward-facing hand was positioned at stomach level, and then opened. The bubble was subsequently dropped and burst immediately on contact. In the second stage, the researcher's hand was soaked in the solution and the experiment was repeated. This time, the bubble stayed as a dome on the researcher's hand for a few seconds and then burst. In the final stage, a cotton glove was placed on the researcher's hand, and the experiment was repeated. The bubble bounced repeatedly. Upon reflection, this experiment proved that the optimal way to make a bubble bounce is to wear a cotton glove.

3.3.A

Answer the following:

1. How is the information organized in the above paragraph? (Underline the phrases that help to organize the paragraph).
2. Is the paragraph written in the passive or the active voice? Why?
3. Is the experiment described above easy to replicate (perform again)? Why or why not?

3.4 Language

A paragraph which provides information is referred to as an *informational* paragraph.

An *informational* process paragraph is written in the *passive voice*:

e.g. the following apparatuses were used / the solution was made / a bubble was blown

In an **active sentence**, the subject (which is also called the "agent") performs the action.

Subject / Agent	Active verb	Object
I	tested	the theory
We	discovered	many variables

In a **passive sentence**, the subject and the agent are not the same.
The passive voice places emphasis on the object of an active sentence.
Naming the agent is sometimes unnecessary.

Subject	Passive verb [be + past participle]	Agent
The theory	was tested	[by the researcher]
Many variables	were discovered	[by the team]

3.4.A

In the paragraph below, use the correct form of the verbs to fill the gaps.

Nuclear reactors ____________ (**1. produce**) electricity from a process called fission, which refers to the process of splitting uranium atoms. This ____________ (**2. create**) by blasting the central section (i.e. the nucleus) of a uranium isotope (235 U) with neutrons. As a neutron collides with a nucleus, it ____________ (**3. rupture**), thereby discharging energy. In turn, this energy ____________ (**4. heat**) water that ____________ (**5. surround**) control rods. These are ____________ (**6. make**) from elements such as boron, silver, indium, and cadmium. The next stage ____________ (**7. occur**) in a heat exchanger, into which the hot water ____________ (**8. pump**), and is turned into steam. In the final stage, a turbine ____________ (**9. drive**) by the steam, which ____________ (**10. propel**) the generator to produce electricity.

The language of **cause-and-effect** can also be used to describe parts of a process.

❖ **because + subject + verb (dependent clause)**

Example: *Because the Skywalk's planned height was 4600 feet (1402 meters), cranes had to be specially constructed for the project.*

❖ **-ing clause**

Example: *High winds were an issue, causing the cranes to sway and hitches for inspection abseilers.*

❖ **because of / as a result of + noun phrase**

Example: *Because of the jagged rock face, many other challenges were anticipated.*

❖ **due to**

Example: *Many construction workers suffered from vertigo due to the enormous height.*

❖ **so + that + clause**

Example: *Robust reinforced glass was manufactured so that it could withstand all the weight.*

❖ **therefore / consequently / as a result / hence + clause**

Example: *Some visitors fail to anticipate the scale; as a result, they are too fearful to walk.*

3.4.B

The diagram below represents the process by which a tornado is produced. Complete sentences 1-14 using the *active* or *passive* verb form. The first sentence has been completed for you.

1. Warm moist air and cool dry air *converge*.
2. Moist air ____________ below dry air.
3. Atmospheric instability ____________.
4. On a hot day, the moist air ____________ in temperature.
5. The moist air ____________ through the dry cool air.

6. An updraft 16/18 km high ____________.
7. The moisture in the air ____________.
8. Thunderstorm clouds ____________.
9. Static electricity ____________.
10. The updraft ____________ the Coriolis force.
11. The thundercloud core ____________ with the updraft.
12. A funnel cloud ____________.
13. It ____________ towards the ground.
14. Once contact ____________ a tornado ____________.

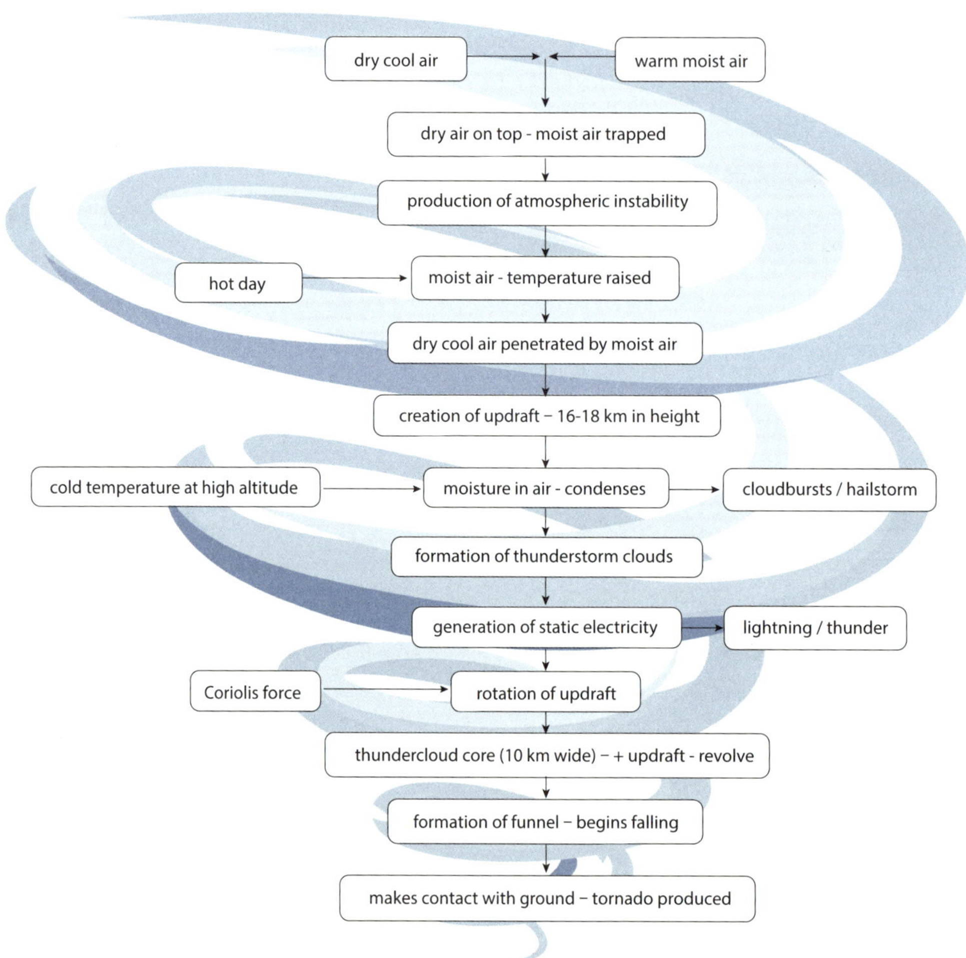

3.4.C

Join each pair of sentences below using the structure, word, or expression in parentheses. The numbers reference the sentences in 3.4.B.

You may need to alter the original sentences.

a. 1 and 2 (-ing clause) Example: *Warm moist air and cool dry air converge, trapping the moist air below the dry cool air.*

b. 2 and 3 (hence) ______________________

c. 4 and 5 (because) ______________________

d. 5 and 6 (-ing clause) ______________________

e. 7 and 8 (due to) ______________________

f. 8 and 9 (as a result of) ______________________

g. 10 and 11 (consequently) ______________________

h. 11 and 12 (as a result) ______________________

i. 12 and 13 (consequently) ______________________

j. 12 and 14 (due to) ______________________

3.4.D

Rewrite the sentences from 3.4.C as a paragraph, adding any *sequence expressions* from 3.2.A that you think may be suitable.

____

The prepositions *by* and *until* play an important part in describing processes.

When describing a chronological process (a series of time-ordered events) we often use these prepositions.

❖ until

Example: *The surface is completely dry until the appearance of condensation on a cold day.*

- the above describes a continuous action that occurs (or is in motion).
- *until* signals the stopping point of the action.

- *until* can also be used as a conjunction.

Example: *The surface is completely dry until, on a cold day, condensation starts to appear.*

❖ by

Example: *All students need to complete their paragraph assignment by 6 pm tomorrow.*

- *by* - *usually* used to describe a deadline of some kind.
- *by* - describes the absolute deadline for the completion of the action.

❖ by the time (phrase)

Example: *All the tickets had been sold by the time the Skywalk was completed.*

- states what has already happened, at the same time that something else happens.

3.4.E

Complete these sentences by inserting *by*, *until*, or *by the time* into the gaps:

1. The test subjects must complete their screening ____________ Friday at noon.
2. ____________ all the participants arrived, the experiment was already set up.
3. It was imperative for the Skywalk to open ____________ the deadline date.
4. This question has mostly been ignored by researchers and scientists ____________ now.
5. The infants in this study did not walk ____________ they were 18 months old.
6. Mold had spread throughout the petri dish ____________ the samples were collected.

The conjunctions *when* / *as* used with *which* also play an important function when describing processes.

In particular, they can be used to create more *cohesion* as illustrated below:

Example: *Pressure is applied to the pedal. At the same time, the chain rotates around the gear. This allows the bicycle to move forward.*

Example: *As pressure is applied to the pedal, the chain rotates around the gear, which allows the bicycle to move forward.*

❖ when + which

Example: *When the faucet is opened, internal pressure is released, which allows water to flow outward.*

Example: *When the acidic solution is added, a reaction occurs, which turns the litmus paper red.*

- *when* – means at or during the time that.
- *which* – used to refer to something previously mentioned when introducing a clause with more information.

❖ as + which

Example: *As cloudbursts or hailstorms are created from condensation from the air, the thunderstorm clouds produce static electricity, which produces thunder and lightning.*

Example: *There were many alterations that had to be made as the engineers finalized the design, which required rigorous cross-checking to avoid errors.*

- *as* – indicates that something occurs during the time when something is taking place.

3.4.F

Combine the sentences below to create a single sentence using *when* / *as* + *which*.

1. Moist air gets trapped below cool, dry air. Immediately afterwards, the hot temperature causes the moist air to heat up and rise. It then surges through the cool air and ascends swiftly in a violent updraft.
2. An updraft starts to rotate. Immediately afterwards, a large portion of the inside of a thundercloud starts to turn along with the updraft. The resulting vortex, which is called a mesocyclone, generates smaller, compact vortices or funnel clouds at the foot of the thundercloud.

3.5 Reading

3.5.A

With your partner(s), discuss the following questions:

1. What is Alzheimer's disease?
2. How much do you know about the human brain and how it functions?
3. What are some different parts and functions of the brain?

3.5.B

Read the paragraph and reflect on answers to questions 1-5 that follow.

How Alzheimer's Disease Spreads Throughout the Brain

Alzheimer's is a debilitating brain disease which ends with the death of the patient. It affects one in ten people over the age of 65. The disease develops gradually, as plaques[1] and tangles[2] , two abnormal protein fragments, amass in the brain and kill brain cells. The process begins in the brain's hippocampus[3], the region of the brain in which memories initially develop. Over a period of many years, the plaques and tangles slowly break down the hippocampus. As a result, forming new memories becomes very difficult. During this stage, the Alzheimer's patient is unable to remember events as recent as a few hours earlier. From the hippocampus, the plaques and tangles then spread into the language-processing region of the brain, which makes it difficult for the patient to form even simple sentence structures. Next, the disease affects logical thought as it edges toward the front of the brain. Hence, over time, the patient can no longer solve problems or make plans. After that, the patient's emotions are affected as the plaques and tangles then take over the part of the brain which regulates emotions. Consequently, the patient's moods and feelings can no longer be controlled. The disease subsequently spreads further to the area of the brain which processes sight, sound, and smell. In this stage, Alzheimer's ravages a person's senses and can cause hallucinations. Eventually, the plaques and tangles invade the back of the brain and erase a person's most precious memories. A patient becomes unstable near the end as balance and coordination skills are severely diminished. The final stage occurs when the disease destroys the ability of the patient to breathe, resulting in death. Alzheimer's develops over an average of eight to ten years as the patient's symptoms slowly move from moderate memory lapses to death. The disease is unrelenting and, at present, unstoppable. Raising awareness of Alzheimer's within the community will improve care, reduce stigma, and help search for better treatment.

1. abnormal clusters of protein fragments which are built up between nerve cells
2. dead and dying nerve cells which are made up of twisted strands of another protein
3. the part of the brain where memories are first formed

Process Paragraph Discussion Questions.

1. What is the purpose of the first sentence in the paragraph?
2. What are some different transition words in this paragraph which refer to the sequence of events?
3. What are some different words or expressions in this paragraph which refer to the duration of events?
4. Consider this sentence near the end of the paragraph:
   "Alzheimer's develops over an average of eight to ten years as the patient's symptoms slowly move from moderate memory lapses to death."
   What is the purpose of this sentence within the context of the overall paragraph?
5. What is the purpose of the concluding sentence?

3.5.C

Based on the previous reading, reflect on answers to the additional discussion questions that follow.

1. Find and explain examples of parallelism in this paragraph. (see 4.4)
2. Find and explain examples of appositives in this paragraph. For any examples that you find, identify the appositive as either essential or nonessential.
3. Find and explain examples of adjective clauses in this paragraph. For any examples that you find, identify the adjective clause as either essential or nonessential.
4. Consider the following sentence from this paragraph:
   "From the hippocampus, the plaques and tangles then spread into the language-processing region of the brain, which makes it difficult for the patient to form even simple sentence structures."
   What does the word "which" specifically refer to?

3.6 Writing

Below you can see an image of a laser printer.

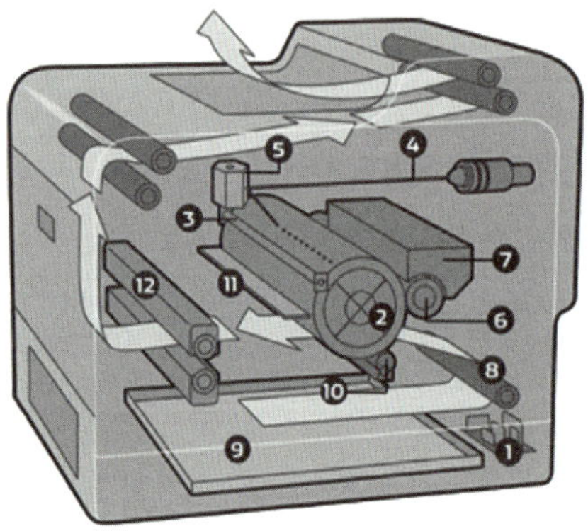

The numbers in the image are labeled as follows.

1. control circuitry
2. imaging drum
3. charging roller
4. laser scanning unit
5. rotating mirror
6. developer roller
7. toner hopper
8. paper roller
9. paper tray
10. supply roller
11. cleaning blade
12. fuser

3.6.A

After viewing the above image and considering the labels above, write an informational process paragraph. The paragraph has been started for you.

How a Laser Printer Works

A laser printer uses electrical attraction and repulsion to print text and images on paper. It consists of several parts: ______________________________

3.6.B

The sentences below represent a sample paragraph which is not in the correct order. With a partner decide on the *correct* sequence by placing the correct sequence number next to each letter.

a. A laser printer uses electrical attraction and repulsion to print text and images on paper. It consists of several parts: …
b. When the laser beam from the laser scanning unit meets the mirror, …
c. In order to print something on paper, these components follow a tightly controlled sequence of steps.
d. … today, it is difficult for us to imagine life without it.
e. … a control circuitry, an imaging drum, a charging roller, a laser scanning unit, a rotating mirror, a toner hopper, and a fuser.
f. … and gives its charge to the drum, …
g. … thereby infusing the surface of the drum with uniform negative charges.
h. … and transmits the interpreted data to the rotating mirror, …
i. … which makes it rotate and stop at the correct angle.
j. … a laser printer can print text or images much faster than printers from the past; …
k. First, a charging roller, which has negative electric charges on its surface, rotates in contact with an imaging drum, …
l. … and the toner forms the printed text and images on it …
m. Next, the control circuitry interprets data from a computer …
n. Then, the charge of the part that is hit by the split beam is changed to a positive charge by the light.
o. … it is split and hits the imaging drum.
p. … because the toner hopper has a negative charge.
q. … as the paper has positive charges as it enters the printer.
r. After this, the toner hopper is attached to the section of the drum that has a positive charge …
s. At this moment, a sheet of paper rolls under the drum …
t. Finally, the ink remains on the surface of paper by heat from the fuser.
u. … by using an electrical force, …
v. In short, …

3.6.C

The sample paragraph below has been arranged in the correct order. Read the paragraph and reflect on the questions that follow.

How a Laser Printer Works

A laser printer uses electrical attraction and repulsion to print text and images on paper. It consists of several parts: a control circuitry, an imaging drum, a charging roller, a laser scanning unit, a rotating mirror, a toner hopper, and a fuser. In order to print something on paper, these components follow a tightly controlled sequence of steps. First, a charging roller, which has negative electric charges on its surface, rotates in contact with an imaging drum, and gives its charge to the drum, thereby infusing the surface of the drum with uniform negative charges. Next, the control circuitry interprets data from a computer and transmits the interpreted data to the rotating mirror, which makes it rotate and stop at the correct angle. When the laser beam from the laser scanning unit meets the mirror, it is split and hits the imaging drum. Then, the charge of the part that is hit by the split beam is changed to a positive charge by the light. After this, the toner hopper is attached to the section of the drum that has a positive charge because the toner hopper has a negative charge. At this moment, a sheet of paper rolls under the drum and the toner forms the printed text and images on it as the paper has positive charges as it enters the printer. Finally, the ink remains on the surface of paper by heat from the fuser. In short, by using an electrical force, a laser printer can print text or images much faster than printers from the past; today, it is difficult for us to imagine life without it.

》Questions

1. Why is 'a' and 'an' used with the nouns charging roller and imaging drum?
2. Where might you insert this defining adjective clause in the paragraph?
   '... that is more commonly known as a photoreceptor drum' ...
3. Can you think of a more appropriate way to say '*gives its charge to*'?
4. Can you think of a more appropriate way to say: '*Then, the charge of the part that is hit by the split beam is changed to a positive charge by the light*'?

5. Why is the passive voice used in '<u>is split</u>' but not in '<u>paper rolls</u>'?
6. Where would you insert this adjective clause?
   … , *which includes the ink particles,* …

In this chapter, you have seen some of the expressions below in earlier exercises. They have been arranged in the sample paragraph below to provide you with an *example* of a *model process paragraph*.

The Coiling Dragon Cliff Skywalk: A Landmark of Modern Engineering

The construction of the Coiling Dragon Cliff Skywalk, located in China, involved complicated and occasionally risky procedures. Cranes had to be specially constructed in advance due to the Skywalk's anticipated height of 4600 feet (1402 meters). Robust reinforced glass was also manufactured so that it could withstand all the weight. Once these essential tasks were completed, the next design phase could proceed. To begin with, sensors and cameras were used to observe the weather in the area and collect data about it. It was quickly realized that high winds were an issue, causing the cranes to sway precariously. In addition to this, because of the jagged rock face, many other challenges were anticipated. However, it was imperative for the Skywalk to open by the deadline date. Thus, during the initial design phase, the Skywalk was modeled to visualize its physical form, structure, and appearance. Before the actual construction began, every component was measured to fit the exact specifications. When measuring, many construction workers suffered from vertigo due to the extreme height. While building, it was important to accurately sort each section into the proper order. Subsequently, every component was labeled with a numbering system. At this point, it was difficult to predict how long constructing the Skywalk would take; in time, the Skywalk was constructed over a period of 6 months. Lastly, the structure was rigorously tested. There were many alterations that had to be made, as the initial tests revealed a few irregularities which required urgent attention. The Skywalk did not open until all safety regulations were met. After a final push to reach full compliance, the Skywalk was opened on time. In sum, the construction process was both complex and risky, but due to conscientious planning and implementation, the Dragon has become a landmark of modern engineering.

Writing Your Process Paragraph

- Now that you have completed Chapter 3, it is time for you to think about the process paragraph that you will write for your assignment.
- You are free to choose any process to write about that relates to engineering, science, or social science. Here are some example topics:
    - *How an airplane flies*
    - *The optimal method for reducing stress*
- Prior to writing your process paragraph, you should discuss your chosen topic with your instructor to ensure that it adequately meets the assignment requirements. You should also follow the specific formatting / evaluating criteria given to you by your instructor.
- Before you start drafting, you should go through the pre-writing process and create a clear outline that shows the coherence (logical connection) of each part of the stages in the process you are writing about.
- After you have created your rough draft, use the revision check list below to make editorial changes.

Revision Checklist

Did you ...

☐ create a clear/concise topic sentence to present the process?

☐ use sequencing expressions to describe specific stages of a process? (see 3.2.A)

☐ use the passive/active voice where appropriate?

☐ use specific verbs connected to engineering or social science disciplines?

☐ join simple sentences in a similar way to 3.4.B and 3.4.C?

☐ use *because of* + noun phrase?

☐ use *therefore/consequently/as a result* + clause to make compound sentences?

☐ use '*until*' to signal the stopping of an action?

☐ use '*by*' to signal the deadline for the completion of the action?

☐ use '*when*', '*as*', and '*which*' to create more cohesion?

☐ write a concluding sentence which reflects upon the process you have described?

4 The Comparison/Contrast Paragraph

How to compare and contrast two concepts or objects

Learning Outcomes:

- to describe similarities and differences
- to learn common verbs and transitional expressions
- to understand the purpose of a comparison and a contrast
- to understand parallelism
- to critique a comparison/contrast paragraph
- to write about comparisons/contrasts with a formal academic style

4.1 Description

The photos below are three different animals (a beaver, a duck-billed platypus, and a duck, from left to right).

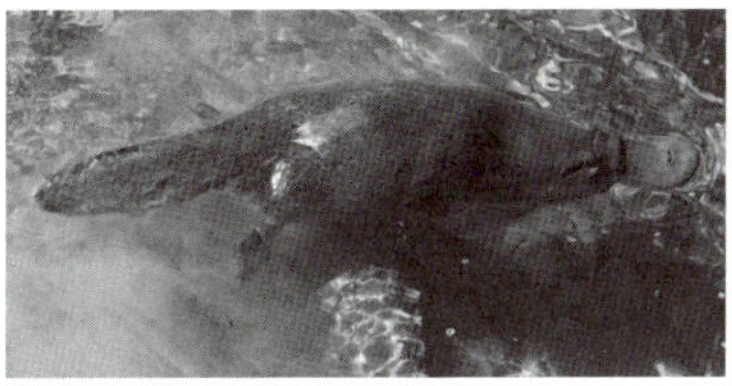

4.1.A

With your partner(s), describe *a minimum of three similarities and three differences* of a platypus with the other two animals.

The duck-billed platypus is a small, amphibious mammal. Its notability within the animal kingdom originates from its strange appearance, which is like a bizarre combination of various animals. As inferred from its name, the duck-billed platypus has a bill like a duck. Moreover, it has many traits similar to a duck. For example, it has webbed feet and lays eggs for reproduction. However, as a member of the mammal class, it also shares many traits with a beaver. The duck-billed platypus has a large flattened tail like a beaver, which is used to propel and brake in the water. Its body is covered with a thick, dark brown, furry coat, which helps repel water to keep its body temperature warm. The duck-billed platypus can also swim well like a beaver, easily gliding through the water to find food.

4.2 Vocabulary

The following are common expressions that are used with comparison and contrast writing in engineering, science, or social science disciplines.

Similarities			
resemble	fit	match	equate
analogize	emulate	approach	approximate
analogous to	the same as … as	as … as	look like
similar	both … and	agree	alike
Differences			
differ	contrast	conflict	disagree
distinguish	different from	differentiate	unlike
dissimilar	not as … as		

When describing similarities and differences in engineering, science, or social science disciplines, the following are a list of possible words/phrases to *communicate transition*.

Similarities			
in the same way	by the same token	likewise	in similar fashion
similarly	also	in the same manner	accordingly
equally			
Differences			
but	despite	however	in another way
nevertheless	conversely	yet	in contrast
on the other hand	in spite of	on the contrary	though
after all	on the contrary	otherwise	nonetheless
while	whereas		

4.2.A

Below are two figures and a table which present similarities and differences between animal and plant cells. Look at the figures and the table and complete the sentences which follow with the suggested expression in parenthesis. After you are finished, write four sentences of your own.

Plant Cell

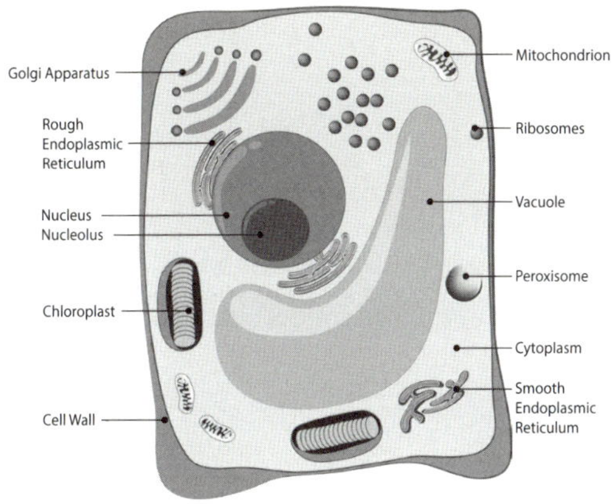

Animal Cell

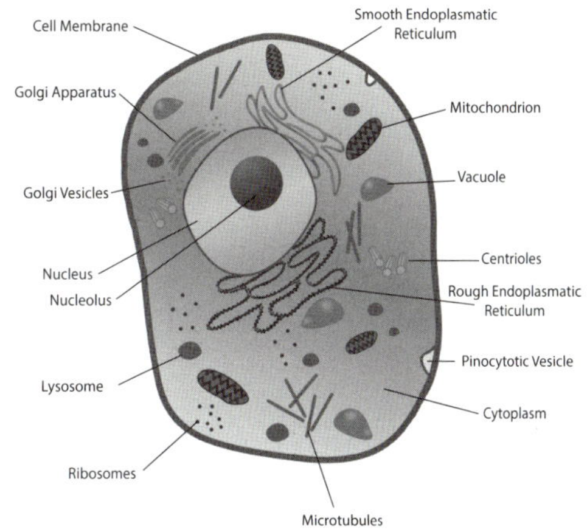

Organelles	Animal Cell	Plant Cell
cell wall	absent	present
shape	round	rectangular
cytoplasm	present	present
chloroplast	absent	present
ribosomes	present	present
mitochondria	present	present
Golgi apparatus	present; few but large	present; many but small

1. The presence of the cell wall *distinguishes plant cells from animal cells.*
2. Animal cells are round, ______________________________ (while).
3. Animal cells, one of the representative higher eukaryotic cells, contain the Golgi apparatus as a secretory organ; ______________________________ (similarly).
4. Plant and animal cells both include the Golgi apparatus. ______________________________ (however).

5. Mitochondria produce the energy currency in animal cells. ______________________ ____ (in similar fashion)
6. ___________________________ (as), they are also present in some lower plants. ____
7. ____
8. ____
9. ____
10. ____

4.2.B

With your partner(s), brainstorm two things that have both similarities and differences, then complete the following table with three similarities and three differences.

Topic		
Similarities		
Differences		

4.2.C

Write three sentences that describe similarities brainstormed in 4.2.B and three sentences that describe differences brainstormed in 4.2.B by using comparison/contrast expressions from 4.2. Use the example below as a model.

Example: *Dogs use their tongues like a scoop to lift and pull water into their mouths; cats, on the other hand, flick water up and catch the water column in their mouths.*

1. ____
2. ____
3. ____
4. ____
5. ____
6. ____

4.3 Purpose

The main purpose of a *comparison* paragraph is to present similarities of objects or concepts:

e.g. explaining the similarities between an airplane and a helicopter.

Read the comparison paragraph below.

The Similarities Between Plant Cells and Animal Cells

Plant cells share many structural features with animal cells. First of all, both animal and plant cells contain nuclei, which store the genetic materials and serve as the brain of the cell. As the primary genetic material, the DNA in both plant and animal cell carries the genetic information and information about its expression. Plant cells, like animal cells, also include mitochondria. The mitochondria, which are analogous to the power plant of organisms, generate the cell's biological energy through the complicated procedure of oxidation reactions. The last organelle contained in both plant cells and animal cells is the Golgi apparatus. The main function of the Golgi apparatus in animal and plant cells is to transport, modify, and package proteins and lipids into vesicles for delivery to target organelles. Without the Golgi apparatus, many organelles in the cell cannot function properly. In conclusion, although plants look completely different from animals, they both have the same – or at least similar – organelles, which serve nearly equal functions in both cells.

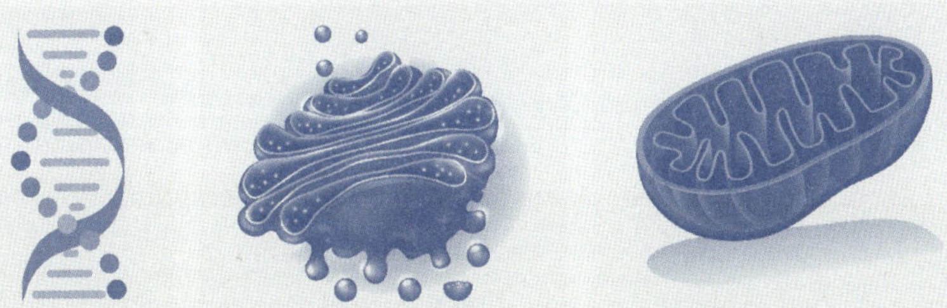

The main purpose of a contrast paragraph is to present the differences between two subjects:

e.g. explaining the differences between an airplane and a helicopter.

Read the contrast paragraph below.

The Differences Between Plant Cells and Animal Cells

Although plant cells and animal cells have many characteristics in common, they also have many distinct features. The outermost area of the plant cells is enclosed within the cell walls. This rigid extracellular structure protects plant cells. Due to the rigidity of the cell wall, plant cells have a rectangular shape. The last but most important characteristic of plant cells is that they have unique organelles called chloroplasts. Chloroplasts in plant cells absorb light energy from the sun and transform it into sugars through a process called photosynthesis. However, animal cells do not have rigid cell walls in the outmost part of the cell, and thus the shape of the cell is round and flexible. Animal cells are also absent of chloroplast. Therefore, animal cells cannot survive on their own since they cannot generate energy independently. These seemingly small differences in the cells of plants and animals ultimately lead to great differences and create a symbiotic reliance on each other for survival.

4.3.A

Answer the following:

1. What is the purpose of the first and second paragraphs above? Explain the specific reasons for your answer.
   a) to present similarities, or
   b) to present differences
2. Underline the similarities that are discussed in the comparison paragraph.
3. Underline the differences that are discussed in the contrast paragraph.
4. How many supporting points are discussed in each paragraph?
5. How is the information about the supporting points in each paragraph organized?
6. What transitional expressions are used in each paragraph?

After the topic sentence, the supporting points are discussed in the body. The point-by-point and block-by-block patterns represent the two main organizational patterns of supporting points.

A. Point-by-point pattern

The point-by-point organizational pattern discusses one supporting point at a time.

B. Block-by-block pattern

The block-by-block pattern organizes all the supporting points of a subject (an object or concept) in one block and those of the second subject in the other block.

In the comparison paragraph above, the supporting points are discussed point by point, whereas the contrast paragraph explains all the supporting points about plant cells in one block, and then explains the supporting points about animal cells in the second block.

4.4 Language

Parallelism, or parallel structure, refers to the use of the same grammatical structure or word patterns for multiple ideas with the same level of importance. Parallelism works at all levels (words, phrases, clauses, and sentences). Faulty parallelism can hinder the readers' comprehension and also can result in poor writing style.

Examples of parallelism	Examples of faulty parallelism
Seeing is believing.	*Seeing is to believe.*
Out of sight, out of mind.	*Out of being seen, out of mind.*

❖ Parallel Structures

Word level

Nouns	Verbs	Adjectives	Adverbs
beakers glassware computers	examines investigated look into	inquisitive attentive thoughtful	inquisitively attentively thoughtfully

Phrase level

	Gerundive phrases	Infinitival phrases	Prepositional phrases
Parallelism	thinking drinking	to support to turn up	in the beaker on the scale
Faulty Parallelism	thinking to drink	to support turned up	in the beaker the scale

Clause level

	Clauses
Parallelism	*because* the temperature slowly cools down *as* two solutions are mixed
Faulty Parallelism	*because* the temperature slowly cools down <u>with</u> two solutions

Parallelism is required when:

1. listing items
2. conjoining words, phrases, or clauses with a coordinating conjunction (for, and, nor, but, yet, so)
3. using words, phrases, or clauses with a correlative conjunction (both… and, not only… but also…, neither… nor, either… or, whether… or, not… but)
4. comparing words, phrases, or clauses with a comparing word (than, as, to)

❖ Faulty parallelism

Example: *Participants were asked to be seated, watching the computer screen, and answered the questions.*

❖ Parallelism

Example: *Participants were asked to be seated, to watch the computer screen, and to answer the questions.* (*to + infinitive phrases*)

Note: *Because of the grammatical rules of parallelism, the sentence above can also be written as follows:*

Example: *Participants were asked to be seated, watch the computer screen, and answer the questions.* (*infinitive phrases*)

Example: *Participants sat down in their chairs, watched the computer screen, and then answered the questions.* (*verb phrases*)

The following has been extracted and adapted from: Wells, D.L., Coleman, D., & Challis, M.G. (2006). *Applied Animal Behaviour Science*, *100*, 327-332.

4.4.A

In the paragraph below, fill in the gaps by using the correct form of the words or phrases in brackets.

A Note on the Effect of Auditory Stimulation on the Behaviour and Welfare of Zoo-Housed Gorillas

Gorillas are one of our closest-living relatives, sharing many of the same physiological and __________ (**1. anatomy**) features. They may thus be expected to react to their auditory environment, and perhaps even __________ (**2. gain**) some of the benefits that humans accrue from auditory cues. This study aimed to determine whether gorillas, like humans or other primates, respond to their auditory environment and __________ (**3. elucidate**) the value of auditory stimulation as a method of enrichment for these animals.

4.4.B

Look at the following picture and table and correct the sentences' faulty parallelism. The first sentence has already been corrected for you.

VS.

Nutrients	Sweet potato	Potato
Calories	0.86 kcal/g	0.77 kcal/g
Fat	1.0 mg/g	1.0 mg/g
Potassium	3.37 mg/g	4.21 mg/g
Carbohydrate	200 mg/g	170 mg/g
Fibers	30 mg/g	22 mg/g

1. The table summarizes both sweet potatoes' and potatoes' nutrition facts.
2. People would rather eat potatoes than to eat sweet potatoes because they think sweet potatoes' are higher in calories than potatoes.
3. Many people do not know where to find the nutrition facts and how they should read them.
4. The nutrition facts label can easily be found in the package; in addition to the calorie information, it contains the information on the kinds of nutrients and how much of them is included.
5. When reading and compare the labels, people should be attentive to the information about the serving size and how many times each container can serve.

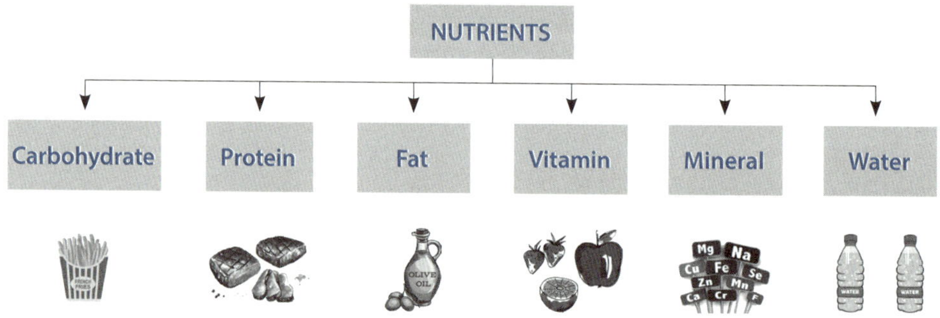

4.5 Reading

4.5.A

With your partner(s), discuss the following questions:

1. What is an engine? What does it do for a car?
2. What are the two different types of car engines?
3. What are the similarities and differences between both types of car engines?

4.5.B

Read the paragraph and discuss the seven questions that follow.

Diesel vs. Gasoline Engines

Most modern cars use either diesel or gasoline engines, both of which convert the chemical energy into mechanical energy to move the wheels of a car forward through a series of combustions. Although the two engines operate on the basis of four strokes of intake, compression, ignition, and exhaust, key differences result from how the four strokes are executed. During the intake stroke, gasoline engines pull in air and mix it with fuel, while diesel engines intake only air. Once compressed, the mixture of fuel and air is ignited by spark plugs in gasoline engines. On the contrary, in diesel engines, fuel is injected into compressed air, and the heated air due to compression then ignites fuel without spark plugs, which is called self-ignition. In gasoline engines, the compression ratios of fuel and air are relatively low in order to protect the engines, which is generally associated with lower energy efficiency. However, diesel engines are more energy efficient because of high compression ratio. These details of the four strokes reveal highly unique characteristics of each engine type.

〉Comparison/Contrast Paragraph Discussion Questions

1. What is the purpose of the first sentence in the paragraph?
2. Where is the topic sentence? What is primarily discussed in the paragraph: similarities or differences?
3. How is the information organized?
4. What are some different transition words in this paragraph which refer to the characteristics of the two different types of car engines?
5. How many subjects are discussed in the paragraph?
6. What is the purpose of the concluding sentence?
7. Can you find any examples of parallelism in this paragraph?

4.6 Writing

Write your own comparison or contrast paragraph. You can go back to one of the previous sections and write about it. For example, you can write a comparison or contrast paragraph about a platypus and a beaver.

❖ Paragraph Structure

A comparison/contrast paragraph begins with a *topic sentence*. Think of a topic sentence that encapsulates the whole paragraph.

The *supporting sentences* should discuss details about the topic sentence. Choose one of the two organizational patterns. Think of three or four supporting points for your selected topic to be compared or contrasted.

The *concluding sentence* wraps up the paragraph. Instead of restating the topic sentence, try to end the paragraph with a fresh, original idea that arises naturally out of the ideas from the paragraph.

Writing Your Comparison/Contrast Paragraph

- This is the end of Chapter 4. It is now time for you to think about the comparison/contrast paragraph that you will write for your assignment.
- You can focus on either the similarities or differences of your selected topic.
- You can organize your paragraph point-by-point or block-by-block.
- Here are some example topics that you may wish to write about:
    - *The differences between the drinking method of cats and dogs*
    - *The similarities between the flying behavior of helicopters and dragonflies*
- Before you start drafting, you should go through the pre-writing process and create a clear outline that shows the coherence (logical connection) between each stage of the comparison/contrast you are writing about.
- After you have created your rough draft, use the revision checklist below to make editorial changes.

Revision Checklist

Did you ...

☐ create a clear/concise topic sentence to present the comparison/contrast?

☐ use an appropriate organizational structure to present the comparison/contrast?

☐ create a clear/concise concluding sentence to wrap up the comparison/contrast?

☐ use expressions to describe similarities/differences?

☐ use transitional expressions to sequence similarities/differences?

☐ use parallel structure correctly?

Unit 2

The Scientific Research Paper

5. Research Design
6. Introduction
7. Methodology
8. Results
9. Discussion/Conclusion
10. Abstract

5 Research Design

Setting up the foundation and requisite components of a scientific research project

Learning Outcomes:

- to understand the purpose of a scientific research study
- to learn about different kinds of scientific evidence
- to learn about the different types of scientific research studies/papers
- to understand the link between a scientific research study and paper
- to learn about the specific components of scientific research design
- to brainstorm ideas for a scientific research project

5.1 Overview

Thus far, we have exclusively focused on paragraph writing. As you have learned, writing is a step-by-step process, with each step building upon the one that preceded it. The next step, which is the central aim of the remainder of this textbook, is to build upon our prior knowledge of paragraph writing to attempt a writing project much larger in scope: a scientific research paper.

All scientific research papers follow the same structure and include similar components. While the content of the papers can vary a great deal, the structure will not. You will learn about the structural components of a scientific research paper in the remaining chapters in this textbook: the introduction, methodology, results, and discussion/conclusion sections, as well as the abstract.

Before even attempting to write a scientific research paper, though, we first need to understand the principles of research design. Trying to write a research paper without understanding basic design principles would be like trying to build a house without a blueprint. We need to have a proper theoretical foundation in place before we even attempt to build something in the real world; without it, its shaky foundations will inevitably lead to our house crumbling down.

Ultimately, every section in a research paper can be traced back to its original design; moreover, a well-written research should make its design principles very clear to the reader. In this chapter, you will begin to put those design elements in place.

5.2 Purpose

The purpose of every scientific research study is to either provide a solution to a problem or an answer to a basic question about the world that we live in. At its heart, this is the aim of every scientific research project.

Everything that we know about science originally began with the process of simple inquiry. Why does matter fall back to the Earth, rather than just float up into space? How do we know that the Earth revolves around the Sun, and not the other way around? What are the most elemental particles of the physical world that we live in?

Many centuries ago, both scientists and philosophers began to ask basic questions like these, and then set about trying to devise methods for answering them both concretely and discretely. That is one of the main goals of science. Over time, this kind of approach became known as *empiricism*, a branch of philosophy which asserts that everything we know to be true must ultimately be based on sensory perception – that which we see, hear, feel, taste, or smell. This kind of sensory input represents *empirical evidence* for our beliefs about the world.

In the next three subsections (5.2.A, 5.2.B, and 5.2.C), we will consider the different types of evidence that are used to reach conclusions about our research questions. By doing this, we will create a connection between the start of our research project and its end.

5.2.A

With your partner(s), brainstorm basic questions that you can ask about the physical world that we live in. As part of this brainstorming exercise, what kind (or kinds) of empirical evidence would you need in order to answer your questions? What is the specific kind of sensory information that you would need to serve as empirical evidence?

In many of the traditional sciences such as physics, chemistry, or biology, empirical evidence serves as the basis for data-driven analysis. All empirical evidence is measurable in some way, which means it can be quantitatively analyzed. We can measure the speed of an object, for example, or its mass, or the number of decibels that it emits, and that quantitative data can then be used for later statistical analysis. Ultimately, all the conclusions that arise out of scientific research projects must be traced back to quantitative analysis.

In science, empirical evidence represents a reliable foundation of truth. If we say that an object weighs 5 kilograms, that is objectively true and not subject to debate; the statement "this object weighs 5 kilograms" is unambiguous and not dependent on any individual person's subjective perspective. However, there are many other types of valid and quantifiable evidence that we also know to be true, but are either difficult or virtually impossible to measure empirically. Doctors, for example, are very concerned with alleviating the pain that arises from either disease or injury. However, is there a truly empirical method for measuring pain? Surprisingly, there is not. In spite of the enormous advancements in medical knowledge and technology over the past several centuries, an instrument that measures pain empirically and reliably has yet to be invented. Hence, doctors have no choice but to depend on the same method that was probably used by physicians thousands of years ago: *self-reported data*. They ask patients to rate their level of pain on a scale of 1 to 10, and then use the patient's self-reported data as the basis for further diagnosis. And while it is true that pain is certainly a subjective feeling, we can also trust the fact that a patient who rates her level of pain as 2 is clearly suffering less than a patient who rates his level of pain as 8. There must be some kind of objective basis for that self-reported data.

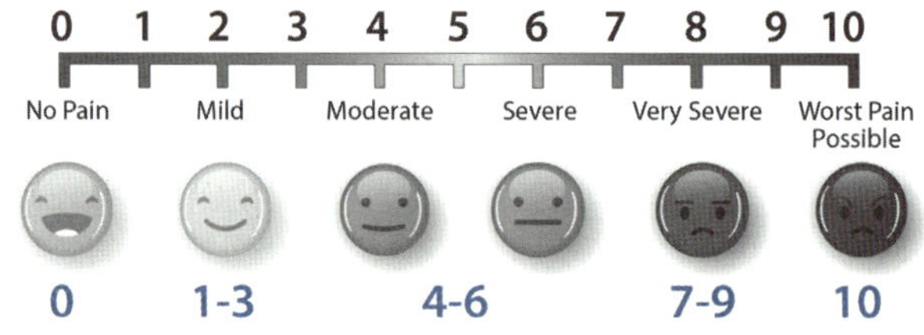

We also might be interested in the subjective preferences of human test subjects and using their self-reported data as the basis for a research study. Later in this book, for example, you will read a number of sections from a scientific research project in which people are asked to report their food preferences. The sum total of people's preferences for different kinds of foods, which are prepared in different ways, can give us valuable information about the optimal way to build a viable nutrition program. Like the pain scale, all we need to do is ask a group of test subjects how much they liked a certain kind of food on a scale of 1 to

10, and then analyze the results. Hence, even subjective feelings or preferences can be a valid source of data.

Pain or food preference both represent abstract concepts that we call *constructs*. In order to measure these constructs, we had to first define them. A simple definition of pain might be "the amount that a person is suffering," while a simple definition of food preference might be "how much a person likes a certain food." These constructs are then *operationalized* so that they can be clearly measured for further analysis. Self-reported data, which is usually measured on a scale of 1 to 10, is the simplest and most straightforward method of operationalizing any given construct.

On a final note, self-reported data is also widely used in survey studies. In a survey study, a researcher will ask test subjects a range of questions, some of which might include the subjects' subjective feelings or preferences. Survey studies can be different from experiments in that the goal of the researchers is simply to gather a range of responses to a series of questions.

5.2.B

With your partner(s), brainstorm different kinds of self-reported data that could be used as the basis for a scientific research project. Areas you might consider include psychology, sociology, nutrition, or medicine.

Thus far, we have considered two types of measurable evidence: empirical evidence and self-reported data. The third type of measurable evidence that we will consider in this book primarily relates to fields such as psychology and sociology, which are both branches of the social sciences.

Psychology, the study of the human mind, investigates the features and cornerstones of the brain in order to better understand the nature of human consciousness and perception. Some aspects of our brains can be empirically measured; for example, we can identify and measure the distinct chemicals that are released when the brain is performing certain functions, or its level of electrical activity across a range of specific tasks. That represents the physical dimension of the brain. However, there is a much more abstract dimension of our brains that most people refer to as the 'mind'. Intelligence and memory, for example, represent two constructs that cannot be measured directly and empirically, and therefore must be defined and operationalized in order to assess these concepts quantitatively.

A person's IQ (which stands for Intelligence Quotient) is supposed to tell us how intelligent they are. Most of us are well-aware that an IQ of 100 is considered average, and a score significantly above 100 would indicate that a person is highly intelligent. IQ is supposed to represent measurable information that we can trust, and which relates to an abstract construct that we call 'intelligence'. However, in order to measure this construct, we had to operationalize it in the real world, and our method of doing so arises directly from how we define this term. If we define intelligence as the ability to solve problems, then our method of operationalizing this definition would be to give test subjects a series of puzzles: mathematical, logical, or visual, for example. However, we might further develop our definition of intelligence by stating it is not only the ability to solve problems, but also to make connections. We might then proceed to add a word analogy section of our intelligence test that asks test subjects to make comparisons (such as *blue is to red as cold is to* ________) and therefore recognize connections between ideas. Ultimately, our intelligence test must be task-based in that anyone who takes the test must perform a series of tasks, which results in some kind of measurable outcome based the number of correct answers the subject had on the exam. Once we have this data, it can be considered empirical because it was a result of observable and measurable behavior.

5.2.C

1. We have just considered the construct of intelligence. In order to quantitatively assess it, we had to define what it is, and then operationalize it so that we can measure and then quantitatively analyze it.

   Consider another crucial construct from psychology: memory. With your partner(s), do the following: (a) Define memory. (b) Think of a research question that you want to answer related to memory. (c) Operationalize your definition so that you can both test a person's memory and answer your research question. Keep in mind that your test must result in a numerical score so that it can later be statistically analyzed.

2. With your partner(s), try to think of other constructs that you could operationalize and then measure. For example, how would you define and operationalize an emotion such as anger or depression? What is the research question that you would want to answer about this construct?

Regardless of its origin, all data is ultimately analyzed through the same set of statistical tests. These tests represent part of the basic structure and systematic approach of every scientific research study. In Chapter 8 of this textbook, you will learn about the different types of standard statistical tests that are used to make meaningful conclusions about the results of your study. From the perspective of a statistical test, data is data; that is true whether the data comes from physics, psychology, or any other field. As long as your research study produces quantitative results, then you will be able to use any of the statistical tests that are explained in this textbook.

Now that we have reviewed the different types of evidence we might find in a scientific research paper, we will now turn our attention to the different types of research papers that scholars typically write.

Scientific papers can fall into two primary categories, although both types of papers are based on research projects. The first is called a *literature review*. The word 'literature' carries a different meaning than its most common usage; we are not referring to the type of writing done by Shakespeare, Dickens, or Hemingway. Literature, in this alternative definition, refers to the set of writing in any academic field or subfields. Physics, chemistry, biology, psychology, and sociology all have their own literature, and the literature within these fields can be further specialized according to specific research areas.

In a literature review, the author seeks to answer a basic question that he or she has about the world, but all of the evidence comes from scientific articles that have been previously published. Literature reviews can be very useful because they provide a summary of all the attempts that have been made to address a specific research question, and might in some cases provide insights and connections to in the existing research that were previously undiscovered or unnoticed. Literature reviews do not, however, create an original set of data.

A *research paper*, on the other hand, is based on an original set of data that has been gathered by the author of the paper. How the author goes about acquiring this data can vary enormously according to a broad range of factors. The author might, for example, form a slightly different question about a well-known topic. Or, perhaps the author's question is not an original one, but the method he or she uses to answer the question is different than any methods previously used in the field. Or, perhaps the author is not interested in originality at all; instead, he or she wishes to replicate an existing research study to see how closely the data matches the original. All of the aforementioned options are completely valid ways of writing a scientific research paper.

It is important to note, though, that research papers will still have some kind of literature review in them; they just won't reference previous studies to the extent that a pure literature review does. It is virtually impossible and, moreover, unprofessional, to not make any mention of the work that has inspired the research study in question.

The sole focus of this textbook is to guide you through the process of writing an original research paper, as you will not be writing a literature review in the textbook. Every component of the research writing process is meant to help you achieve this aim.

To make a final point about your goals with your research study, you should try to keep your questions, and your scientific ambitions, as simple as possible at this point. Your objective is ultimately to write a clear, straightforward scientific research paper. If you are able to accomplish this aim through some kind of groundbreaking and original scientific research study, then congratulations – you are already well ahead of the curve. However, writing a scientific research paper is an extremely difficult and complex process. Be realistic. When forming your topic and your research question, you should ask yourself this basic question before proceeding further: "Am I able to write about this topic and answer this question at a level that is sufficiently clear to the reader?" Always keep your reader's point of view in mind during the research design phase.

5.2.D

Consider the following research purpose statement and answer the questions below.

In our experiment, we conducted laboratory scale testing of industrial eggshell catalysts for the selective hydrogenation of acetylene in order to determine the optimal numerical modeling and performance studies of the advanced TEMKIN reactor.

Can you determine the specific question that is being asked by this research study? How would you proceed with both designing and writing a scientific research paper based on the previous question?

Now, consider this alternative research purpose statement:

In our experiment, we conducted a series of tests to determine the optimal cup material for maintaining a sufficiently hot temperature of coffee.

Again, can you determine the specific question that is being asked in this research study? How would you proceed with both designing and writing a scientific research paper based on the previous question?

5.2.E

Consider these three simple questions as a starting point for a research study:

1. What is the optimal method for insulating a home in order to reduce energy costs?
2. How can we make healthy foods taste better so that people will make better nutritional choices?
3. Can listening to music improve cognitive performance?

All three of these questions will be addressed later in this textbook in samples from various research papers. With your partner(s), explain how you would proceed with both designing and writing a scientific research paper based on the previous questions. In your discussion, explain the specific type of evidence that will be used to answer each of the previous questions, using the concepts you learned in subsections 5.2.A, 5.2.B, and 5.2.C.

Next, write three original research questions with your partner(s). As you have done previously, explain how you would proceed with both designing and writing a scientific research paper based on your question, as well as the type of evidence that would be needed to answer each question.

5.3 Language

In this section, you will review vocabulary from section 5.2, as well as preview vocabulary from section 5.4.

empirical evidence	self-reported	construct
operationalized	literature review	research paper
constant	observational study	independent
dependent	control group	controlled experiment
treatment group	treatment effect	significant effect
null hypothesis	alternative hypothesis	

5.3.A

Complete the sentences with one of the words in the box above.

1. ____________ variables are manipulated by the researcher to see what kind of effect they have on the outcome of an experiment.
2. ____________ variables represent the measurable results of an experiment.
3. Any data that arises out of what we perceive with our senses – that which we can see, hear, or touch, for example – is called ____________.
4. Any data that originates in test subjects giving the researcher information about themselves is called ____________ data.
5. A ____________ is a collection of individual people, animals, organisms, or objects that researchers manipulate in some manner.
6. A ____________ is a collection of individual people, animals, organisms, or objects that represent the baseline of an experiment and is therefore not manipulated.
7. A _______________ is a type of study in which the researchers are manipulating a specific variable in order to test its effects.
8. An ____________ is a type of study in which researchers do not manipulate any variables themselves, and instead watch and record information from the world around them.

9. A ____________ is a specific component of an experiment that does not vary or change.

10. A ____________ is a type of scientific writing that summarizes the research projects related to a specific topic.

11. A ____________ is a type of scientific writing that seeks to answer a specific research question by collecting an original set of data.

12. A ____________ is an abstract concept that researchers are trying to examine and understand better. It must be ____________ in order to produce measurable results.

13. The extent to which a manipulated variable in an experiment influences the result is known as the ____________. If it is large enough, then researchers can confidently state that it had a ____________.

14. A ____________ is a prediction that a variable will not have a noticeable effect on the results.

15. An ____________ is a prediction that a variable will have a noticeable effect on the results.

5.4 Goals and Structure

As we discussed previously, all scientific research studies need to be based on measurable results; in other words, they need to be designed in such a way that they can produce data which gives a clear, objective result which can be further analyzed. Research studies can be broadly classified into two types: *controlled experiments* and *observational studies*. In this section, we will first examine the characteristics of a controlled experiment.

A controlled experiment is the type of research study that normally comes to mind when we imagine a scientific laboratory. Not all laboratories are filled with beakers, tubes, and other assorted glassware, but the one common link shared by every laboratory is that the researcher controls every component and phase of the research process.

5.4.A

With your partner(s), consider the following simple controlled experiment: A new type of soil has been developed which has been injected with a range of minerals from around the world; the soil is a hybrid of local soil and the extra minerals. The developers of this type of soil believe that it can enhance the growth performance of a certain kind of plant. You want to determine whether or not the developer's assertion is really true, so you begin the process of designing a controlled experiment to test this claim. As a way of brainstorming your design, consider the following questions.

1. What is the original research question?
2. What are the individual components of this controlled experiment? For this question, you might include the types of materials needed to perform the experiment, as well as the input you are providing each plant.
3. What is the measurable result of this controlled experiment? In other words, what is the data outcome?
4. What is the method that you will use in order to produce the data outcome?
5. How can you ultimately answer the original research question?

Next, we will turn our attention to the observational study. Unlike a controlled experiment, the researchers seek to merely observe the results of a process that they essentially have no control over. However, as you will see, an observational study still requires a structured scientific approach that has many characteristics in common with a controlled experiment.

There are many types of research projects that work better as observational studies than controlled experiments. The first that we will consider relates to the weather.

5.4.B

The city of San Francisco is well-known for a number of reasons: its natural beauty, its cutting-edge culture, and its diverse cuisine, for example. What many visitors are surprised to learn, though, is that San Francisco's weather patterns can vary enormously within the city, depending on the neighborhood. The Outer Richmond district – a neighborhood which resides very close to the ocean – appears by most accounts to have a much higher fog density than neighborhoods that are further away from the ocean, and the temperature seems to be much lower as well. On the other hand, Portola – a neighborhood which resides far away from the ocean and is close to the southern boundary of the city – almost always appears to be bright and sunny.

With your partner(s), consider the following observational study: You have been asked by the city of San Francisco to determine whether or not there really are substantial differences in the weather patterns in different areas of the city. As a starting point, you decide to monitor three different neighborhoods: the Outer Richmond, Portola, and Haight-Ashbury, which lies roughly at the midpoint between the first two neighborhoods. You want to determine whether or not the claims about differential weather patterns are really true, so you begin the process of designing an observational study to test this claim. As a way of brainstorming your design, consider the following questions.

1. What is the original research question?
2. What are the individual components of this observational study? Are there any specific materials that you will need to conduct the study?
3. What is the measurable result (or, what are the results) of this observational study? In other words, what is the data outcome?
4. What is the method that you will use in order to produce the data outcome?
5. How can you ultimately answer the original research question?

5.4.C

In the previous example, our decision to base our project on an observational study rather than a controlled experiment was essentially driven by a single practical consideration: It is impossible to control the weather. However, ethical considerations might also have an influence.

In the 1950s, medical researchers began to strongly suspect that there was a strong link between smoking and lung cancer; prior to this decade, the information about this link was much more limited and inconclusive. Today we accept this link as fact, but back then, a substantial amount of evidence was needed to prove that smoking and lung cancer were directly connected.

Conducting a controlled experiment to test how strongly smoking and lung cancer are correlated with one another would obviously have been out of the question. With your partner(s), discuss why a controlled experiment for this type of research project would have been completely unethical, and why an observational study was the only possible option in this case. As part of your discussion, explain how you might design this kind of observational study.

The final type of research study you are going to consider is a psychology experiment on video games and aggressive behavior. There has been a longstanding debate in both the media and the field of psychology as to what extent (if any) violent video games lead to aggressive or violent behavior in the real world, and a number of psychological studies have been done in order to answer this question.

5.4.D

With your partner(s), brainstorm the framework for a research project that attempts to determine to what extent (if any) violent video games lead to aggressive or violent behavior in the real world. To help create your design, consider the following questions.

1. What is the original research question?
2. Do you want to design your study as a controlled experiment or an observational study? What are the positive and negative aspects of both?
3. How do you define the constructs 'aggression', 'aggressive behavior', and/or 'violent behavior'?
4. How do you plan to operationalize the construct that you defined in #3? In other words, how will your research study lead to measurable results that are based on your construct definition?
5. What groups are going to be compared in your research study?
6. Related to #4, what is the specific measurable result (or, what are the results) of this study? In other words, what is the data outcome? What specific type of evidence is the data outcome?
7. How can you ultimately answer the original research question?

As part of your brainstorming process in the previous subsections, you were asked to explain the *variables* involved in your research study. Variables can be either independent or dependent. In a research study, an *independent variable* is a variable used by a researcher to determine how strongly it is influencing the results of a study. A *dependent variable*, on the other hand, is a variable that may or may not be influenced by the independent variable. In both controlled experiments and observational studies, the independent variable is pre-selected by the researcher to measure what effect (if any) it has on the dependent variable.

Consider the example from subsection 5.4.A to clarify these concepts. In the soil experiment, the independent variable was the type of soil. The dependent variable was the growth performance of the plant. We can define 'growth performance' in a number of ways, but ultimately, it has to be measurable. Hence, every dependent variable represents the measurable result of the research study.

The only way to determine whether or not Soil X truly leads to higher growth performance of a certain type of plant is to compare it with another soil. Remember that Soil X is a hybrid of the local soil and a range of minerals from around the world. Hence, we can take a sample of the local soil (which we will call Soil L) and use that as the basis of our comparison.

We now have two types of groups established for this experiment. Soil X represents the *treatment group* in this experiment, and Soil L represents the *control group*. The treatment group is the group that receives a specific treatment, and which the researchers are trying to determine whether or not has a significant effect on the results of the experiment. The control group, on the other hand, does not receive any kind of special treatment, and serves as the baseline comparison point for the researchers. The difference between the results of the treatment group and the control group is defined as the *treatment effect*. (Remember that the two types of soil only vary by the extra minerals; hence, the minerals can be said to represent the treatment in this case.) If the treatment effect is particularly large, then we can say that the treatment had a *significant effect*. In other words, we are testing to see whether the treatment has a significant effect on the results (the dependent

variable).

In a controlled experiment, though, we also need to be sure there aren't any other extraneous factors affecting the dependent variable. Hence, we must be certain that all the other factors in the experiment are fixed; these fixed factors are called the *constants* of our experiment. Constants of the soil experiment might include the following:

1. The specific type of plant seed used in the experiment
2. The amount of sunlight given to each plant
3. The amount of water given to each plant
4. The material of the pot that contains the soil

Earlier, we stated that we might define the 'growth performance' of a plant in a number of ways, and we can now return to this idea and define growth performance more specifically. Perhaps we know in advance that each plant is easily capable of reaching a full meter in height in its most mature stage. Hence, we might conduct this type of experiment as a race against the clock, and then try to answer the following research question: How long does it take for the plant from Soil X and the plant from Soil L to reach a height of one meter?

We could, however, fix the time length of the experiment, and instead set the dependent variable as the height of the plant. For example, it might be known that all plants of this type reach their peak height after a maximum of two months. Hence, we could set the experiment at two months in length, and answer the following research question: What is the maximum height for a plant from Soil X and a plant from Soil L?

No matter how we define 'growth performance', we ultimately need to answer the question of whether or not the treatment group was noticeably different from the control group.

5.4.E

The soil experiment is a very straightforward research study based on empirical observation. Because the video game research study relates to human psychology, the characteristics of the study, as well as the measurable results, are a bit more challenging to define. However, we can at least use some of the concepts we now know to better understand this study. With your partner(s), answer the following questions:

1. What are the independent and dependent variables in your video game research study?
2. What is the treatment group? Is there a control group? Are there any other groups in your study?
3. How do you define the treatment effect in your study? How are you going to quantitatively measure the treatment effect?

5.4.F

With your partner(s), consider the following controlled experiment: A pharmaceutical company has invented a new blood pressure medication which, through a series of animal experiments, appears to significantly lower blood pressure. The company now wants to determine whether this medication has a similar effect on humans. Assume that there are no ethical problems with this experiment; the company has already determined that the medication poses no health risks to anyone who takes it.

With your partner(s), answer the following questions:

1. What is the central research question?
2. What is the independent variable?
3. What is the dependent variable?
4. What is the treatment/treatment group?
5. What is the control group?
6. What are the constants?
7. What is the treatment effect?
8. What type of evidence is the data outcome of this experiment?

In re-considering our previous observational study of weather patterns in San Francisco, some of the previous concepts from the previous section apply very well, and others do not.

The independent variable, for example, could be defined as the specific area or neighborhood in San Francisco. We previously only considered three neighborhoods in San Francisco, but we certainly could have included more if we had wanted.

The dependent variable could be defined as a measurable aspect of weather. Temperature would be the easiest to measure, but we might also come up with a method for measuring the fog density. These could represent two different dependent variables in our study that could be considered separately; alternatively, with certain types of statistical tests, we might consider the link between temperature and fog. Examining these kinds of connections is called a correlation study, which will be covered in Chapter 8.

The concepts of the treatment, treatment group, or control group would appear to be more at the discretion of the researcher. While it is possible to come up with some way of defining these concepts within the context of our observational study, we don't necessarily need them. We might be interested in examining whether differences in temperature and/or fog density exist between neighborhoods, but nothing more.

In considering the idea of a treatment effect, though, it might be useful to determine the treatment as the proximity of a given neighborhood to the ocean. As was mentioned previously, neighborhoods that reside closer to the ocean appear to be colder and higher in fog density. We might, then, look at a broad range of neighborhoods in the city, and determine if there is a significant correlation between measurable weather patterns and proximity to the ocean. As proximity to the ocean increases, then, we would expect temperature to decrease and fog density to increase. As proximity to the ocean decreases, we should observe the opposite – temperature should increase and fog density should decrease. However, we would need a valid statistical test to determine whether that connection does in fact exist.

One of the central ideas that we have considered throughout this chapter is the research question; every study needs to begin with one. A *hypothesis* is a statement that makes some kind of truth claim in response to the basic research question. For example, our research question for the soil-related experimental study might be "Does Soil X have a positive effect on the growth performance of plants?"

In response to the previous question, we could make two possible truth claims, which represent two possible hypotheses:

1. Soil X does not have a significantly positive effect on the growth performance of the plant.
2. Soil X has a significantly positive effect on the growth performance of the plant.

The first hypothesis represents the *null hypothesis* of our controlled experiment. In this case, the null hypothesis states that the treatment does not have a noticeable effect on the dependent variable, which in this case is the growth performance of the plant.

The second hypothesis represents the *alternative hypothesis* of our controlled experiment. In this case, the alternative hypothesis states that the treatment has a noticeable effect on the dependent variable; i.e. the growth performance of the plant.

In symbolic notation, we represent the null hypothesis as H_0 and the alternative hypothesis as H_A. It is also possible to use the symbol H_1 for the alternative hypothesis. For consistency's sake, this book will exclusively use H_A. Hence, our two hypotheses would be stated as follows:

H_0: Soil X does not have a significantly positive effect on the growth performance of the plant.

H_A: Soil X has a significantly positive effect on the growth performance of the plant.

Similarly, we could create a pair of hypotheses for our weather pattern-related observational study in San Francisco:

H_0: There are no significant differences in weather patterns among the neighborhoods of San Francisco.

H_A: There are significant differences in weather patterns among the neighborhoods of San Francisco.

Or, we could consider this set of hypotheses for our video game experiment:

H_0: There is no significant difference in aggressive behavior between children who play violent video games and children who do not.

H_A: There is a significant difference in aggressive behavior between children who play violent video games and children do not.

In Chapter 8, you will learn how to formally assess the difference between "significant" and "not significant" in statistical terms.

5.4.G

Write null and alternative hypotheses for the following research questions:

1. Does the new TOEFL preparation class offered by TestPrep increase students' test scores?

   H_0: ______________________________

   ____

   H_A: ______________________________

   ____

2. Does nicotine chewing gum help to reduce smoking?

   H_0: ______________________________

   ____

   H_A: ______________________________

   ____

5.5 Overview of Statistics

After the research project has been completed and the data compiled, a decision then needs to be made about the original hypothesis. Ultimately, we need to decide whether the data outcome in our study supports the null hypothesis or the alternative hypothesis. In order to make this decision, we have to use a set of statistical tools called *inferential statistics*. Looking ahead, this concept will be revisited in Chapter 8, which covers the results section of a scientific research paper. This section will explain the theoretical basis of inferential statistics so that you can have a better understanding of the statistical tests later on. Writing a scientific research paper certainly does not require a deep understanding of all the background and mathematical formulas overviewed in this section. However, for instructors and students who wish to delve more deeply into this area, this section might prove useful.

One of the major foci of statistics is the connection between a population and a sample. A population is defined as the entire set of individual items in a research study, which is always represented as a set of scores. In 5.4.A, for example, you considered a research study that attempted to determine whether a new type of soil (called Soil X) can be claimed to increase the growth performance of a specific type of plant. The population, in this case, is defined as the entire set of this type of plant. We might narrow our scope to define our population as all the plants within a single country, or perhaps a single region in the country, but ultimately, the researchers in this study can only select a sample of plants; i.e. a subset of that population.

The primary goal of gathering and analyzing a sample is that it has some kind of predictive value for the general population. In our soil study example, the researcher's ultimate goal is to manufacture and market Soil X for anyone who wants to grow a specific kind of plant. Statistical analysis of the sample in the study might suggest that the soil has significantly increased the plant's performance, but this conclusion is only meaningful if the sample is an accurate reflection of the entire population. This is one of the central aims of inferential statistics: It seeks to determine how well the results of a sample can be generalized to the larger population. In order to better understand the general population's characteristics, we first need to understand the concept of variance.

Variance refers to the variability of a set of data. All data sets can be described as a range which spans from a minimum to a maximum number. If we sum up all the scores in this range, and then divide the sum by the number of scores in the data set, we attain the *mean* score for the data set, which is often referred to as the average. (As an aside, the *median* and the *mode* – which are defined in Chapter 8 – can also be used to describe an 'average' score, but for the purposes of this textbook we will primarily be using the mean.)

In statistics, many data distributions follow a pattern called a *normal distribution*, also known as a bell-shaped curve. You can see an example of a normal distribution below:

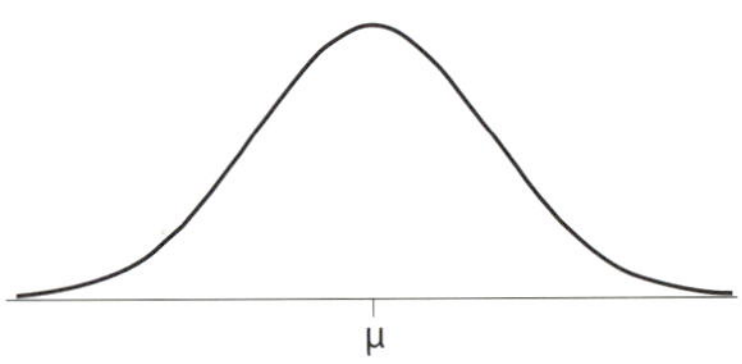

The horizontal axis of this distribution (also called the *x-axis*) shows the range of scores in the distribution. The x-axis also contains the symbol μ, which stands for the mean (or average) score. The vertical portion of the distribution (also called the *y-axis*) shows the total number or *frequency* of scores. Notice that in a normal distribution, the extreme scores in the range are relatively infrequent, while scores that collect around the mean are at the highest level of frequency. If we were to imagine that the distribution above describes the heights of the entire set of plants, then the lower end of the range represents plants which are very short, while the upper end represents plants which are very tall. The height of most of the plants, though, tends to fall in the exact middle of the range.

❖ Variance and Standard Deviation

To return to the concept of variance, each score lies a certain distance from the mean. Any score's distance from the mean is defined as its *deviation*. In order to compute the variance of a data set, we first have to square each score's deviation, then sum up each of the squared deviations. The end result is called the *sum of the squared deviations* and is represented by the following formula:

$$SS = \Sigma(X - \mu)^2$$

In the formula above, SS means "sum of the squared deviations," Σ means "to sum up," X represents a single score, and μ represents the population mean.

Variance is then computed by dividing the sum of the squared deviations by N, the total number of scores in the population, as in the following formula:

$$\sigma^2 = SS/N$$

Our ultimate goal is to find the average distance that any individual score lies from the mean. Because variance is the average squared value of the deviations, the average deviation (which is defined as the *standard deviation*) is defined as the square root of variance, as in the following formula.

$$\sigma = \sqrt{\sigma^2}$$

❖ Z-score

One of the most useful features of standard deviation is that we can use it to describe how far a score resides either above or below the population mean in terms of standard units. To determine this value, we calculate a type of statistic called a *z-score*, which is defined as follows:

$$z = (X - \mu)/ \sigma$$

Let us assume the following values for the plant population: the mean plant height is 2 meters, and the standard deviation is .4 meters. A plant with a height of 2.8 meters would therefore have a z-score of $(2.8 - 2)/.4 = 2$.

We might also consider a completely different distribution of data such as IQ scores. The average IQ of an individual in any given population is 100, and the standard deviation is typically 15. A person with an IQ of 130 would therefore have a z-score of $(130 - 100)/15 = 2$.

As you can see, the plant and the person above have something important in common: their scores (height and IQ, respectively) can both be described as residing two full standard deviations above the population mean. This is considered a rare occurrence, and within the realm of what we call *statistical significance*.

This graph is a normal distribution which shows z-scores ranging from -1.96 to 1.96. Notice that μ, the population mean, is assigned a z-score of 0. This is because if a score is equivalent to the population mean, the z-score will always be computed as 0. For example, a plant that is 2 meters high has a z-score of $(2 - 2)/.4 = 0$. A person with an IQ of 100 has a z-score of $(100 - 100)/15 = 0$.

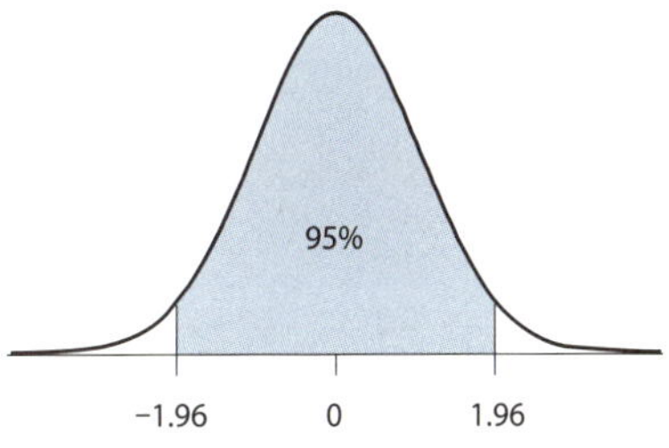

❖ Confidence Interval

Notice that the shaded area of the graph between the two extreme z-score values comprises 95% of its area. In other words, 95% of all scores lie between a z-score of +/–1.96. The other 5% of the scores lie outside this range. Since this graph is perfectly symmetrical, 2.5% of the scores are above 1.96, and 2.5% of the scores are below –1.96.

The 95% range represents our *confidence interval*. If we were to select a random score from this population, we would be 95% confident that the score will fall in the range of z = +/–1.96. To randomly select a score outside this range would be unusual. Any scores that fall outside the range are defined as *statistically significant* within the context of the general population. As another way of thinking about it, an IQ of 130 can be said to be significantly larger than an average IQ of 100 because it lies 2 entire standard distributions above the mean.

Recall our null and alternative hypotheses for the Soil X:

> H_0: Soil X does not have a significantly positive effect on the growth performance of the plant.
>
> H_A: Soil X has a significantly positive effect on the growth performance of the plant.

In our earlier example, we considered a plant that reached a height of 2.8 meters when grown in Soil X. Because the plant height's z-score of 2.0 is just beyond the 1.96 threshold for statistical significance, we can reject the null hypothesis for this study and support the alternative hypothesis. The data supports the viewpoint that Soil X has a significantly positive effect on the growth performance of the plant.

Research studies will often state this conclusion as a *p-value*, which is the probability of finding their observed results on a distribution in which the null hypothesis is true. As the p-value decreases, the researchers' confidence that their results are meaningful increases. In any research study, there is always a small possibility that the results were due to chance. Why did our plant grow to 2.8 meters tall? We might conclude that Soil X played a significant role, but it is possible that the plant's height had nothing to do with the soil at all – perhaps the seed that was chosen for the experiment was a genetic anomaly – and therefore was unrelated to our original hypothesis. Hence, we have to

accept the fact that there is a small probability that our rejection of the null hypothesis was wrong. The z-scores of +/– 1.96 in this test are associated with specific probabilities of 2.5% on the left side of the distribution and 2.5% on the right. Since the probability of attaining a z-score of 2.0 is less than the probability of attaining a z-score of 1.96, then we can state that the p-value for this test is less than 2.5%; or, in mathematical notation, we can write $P < .025$. While there are ways to compute the p-value as a specific number, it is sufficient in scientific writing to state that the p-value is either above or below a certain probability.

This is the starting point for understanding the principles of statistical inference. If a plant grown in Soil X reached a height of 2.8 meters, it would suggest that the plant's height is statistically unlikely in relation to all the other plants in the population. It would be reasonable, therefore, to conclude that the use of Soil X is leading to a significant increase in the plant's height. The stronger growth rate of Soil X plants would not seem to result from chance, although the possibility always exists.

As a final note, the 95% confidence interval is not the only confidence interval used in statistics. Other intervals include 90% (a more lenient confidence interval) and 99% (a stricter confidence interval). For the purposes of this textbook, the 95% confidence interval should be sufficient.

❖ The Distribution of Sample Means and Standard Error

In the previous z-score explanation, notice that we exclusively focused on *single scores* in a population. Research studies, though, almost always relate to samples, which means that *groups* of scores are the actual subject of analysis. The *distribution of sample means* and *standard error* have a direct relationship with the analysis of group scores as a whole.

To continue our plant growth experiment, instead of growing just one plant, we might grow a group of plants in order to collect a valid sample. For this study, we will assume the researcher had the resources to grow 30 different plants using Soil X.

In general, the mean score of larger sample sizes should be closer to the population mean;

this is why researchers try to work with sample sizes that are as large as possible. For this experiment, a sample size of 30 should be sufficient.

Remember that the aim of this study is to determine whether the growth performance of plants grown in Soil X is significantly greater than the average growth performance of plants from the general population. In this case, because we now have a sample of 30 plants, we need some way of comparing our sample mean with the mean of any other 30 plant sample from the general population.

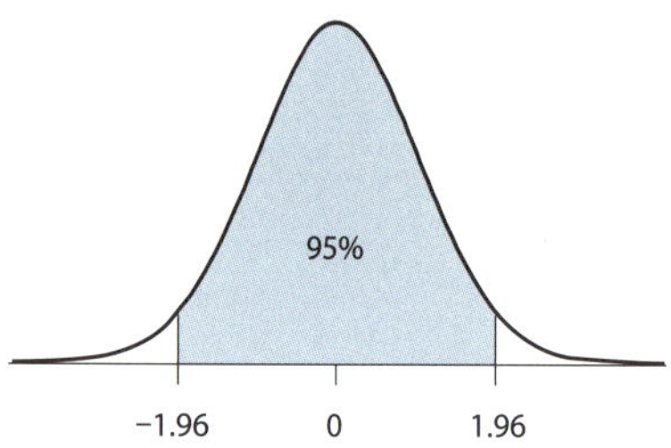

Recall our discussion on the distribution of scores within a population, which tends to form a normal distribution. The distribution of sample mean scores tends to follow the same normal distribution as the general population. Consider the same normal distribution as before: Instead of representing the entire population of plants in which each score represents an individual plant's height, imagine that this graph now represents the mean score for a distribution of plant samples where n = 30. In other words, each score in the distribution represents the average height for a sample of 30 plants. The mean score should be equivalent to the population mean of 2 meters. Hence, we would expect that if we selected a random sample of 30 plants from the population, their mean height would be 2 meters.

How do we define the variance of our sample mean? Instead of computing the standard deviation, we instead have to compute the *standard error* of our sample mean, which is defined as the average deviation of a sample mean from the population mean. To calculate this statistic, we take the square root of the population variance divided by n, the sample size, resulting in the following formula:

$$\sigma_M = \sigma/\sqrt{n}$$

σ_M represents the standard error of the sample, σ represents the standard deviation of the population, and n represents the sample size. Again, the standard error is essentially the same as standard deviation in principle, as it represents the average deviation of a sample mean from the population mean.

❖ Z-score Revisited

Once we determine the standard error of our sample, we can then compute its z-score, which is based on the following formula:

$$z = (M - \mu)/ \sigma_M$$

M represents the sample mean score, μ represents the population mean, and σ_M, as stated before, represents the standard error for the sample.

Consider our sample of plants in which n = 30. The standard error for a sample of size 30 is $.4/\sqrt{30}$. (Remember that the population standard deviation was previously stated as .4 meters.) Hence, $\sigma_M = .073$.

Previously, the single plant grown in Soil X reached a height of 2.8 meters. For our sample of 30 plants, assume the mean height is 2.3 meters – well short of the single plant's height, but still above the population mean. Our z-score is now computed as (2.3 – 2)/.073 = 4.11. In other words, the sample mean is more than 4 standard error units above the population mean, which is well beyond the 1.96 threshold. As in the experiment with the single plant, we can reject the null hypothesis for our study and accept the alternative hypothesis.

Remember that the z-score for our single plant was 2.0. The probability of attaining a z-score of 4.11 is obviously much lower than the probability of attaining 2.0, but it is nevertheless sufficient to state that $P < .025$ for this study. Still, it seems worthwhile to consider the substantial difference between the two z-scores; 4.11 is approximately twice the size of 2.0.

〉 **Question**: Why is the z-score for the sample significantly greater than the z-score for the single plant, even though the single plant's height is 2.8 meters and the sample mean height is comparatively smaller at 2.3 meters?

The answer lies in the power of large samples, and the difficulty in finding large samples that are even slightly above the population mean. Imagine if the researchers had grown 5 plants instead of 30. Now our standard error is $.4/\sqrt{5} = .179$. The sample's z-score, therefore, would be calculated as (2.3 – 2)/.179 = 1.68. Because it falls short of the 1.96 threshold, it cannot be claimed in this case that Soil X significantly increases plant growth performance.

❖ Choosing the Right Statistical Test

Essentially, the purpose for all of the statistical theory that we just covered was to give both instructors and students a better understanding of hypothesis testing and statistical significance. The tools of statistics can be exceedingly complex and varied, but no matter what set of tools we choose, they have one basic function in common: to make a clear and objective conclusion about our original hypothesis rooted in quantitative analysis. All statistical tests share this aim. However, the selection of the exact test we use to assess our hypothesis is far from arbitrary, and must reflect our original research design. It is important to choose the right statistical test in concert with our research design; the test and the design must be tightly integrated with one another.

Students who use this textbook have three primary statistical tests to choose from: a *t-test*, a *one-way ANOVA test*, or a *Pearson correlation test*. These tests have been chosen because they can handle the design of virtually any research project.

Each of these tests will be summarized very succinctly as a more detailed explanation is beyond the scope of this textbook. For further assistance, there are many free tutorials online which can further explain the details of each test such as Khan Academy. There are also many software programs on the market which allow you to input your data and then automatically compute the results, meaning the vast majority of the math will remain hidden.

❖ T-test

The major issue with using a z-score is that it assumes we already know the variance (and therefore the standard deviation) of the population. However, in many cases we do not have access to this information. Fortunately, we can use another statistical test of significance called the t-test – which results in a *t-value* – to circumvent the problem. The t-test is designed to use an *estimated standard error* which is based on our sample data and does not require any knowledge about the entire population. The computation of the t-value is based on the basic principles of the z-score; the mathematical formulas behind both tests look very similar.

Like the z-test, a t-test is a comparison between two groups. There are two primary types of t-tests: *an independent samples* t-test and a *paired sample* t-test. In the first test, two groups that are distinct from one another and consist of different subjects are tested to determine if they are significantly different from one another. The plant soil experiment covered in this chapter is a typical example of an independent samples t-test. On the other hand, a paired sample t-test examines the *same group of test subjects* in two separate instances. In section 5.2.E, for example, you considered a research project that seeks to determine whether or not listening to music improves cognitive performance. You might then proceed to create a group of 20 test subjects and give them a similar (but not exactly the same) mathematical exam on two different days. On the first day, your test subjects take the exam in a room that is completely silent. On the second day, your test subjects – again, the same test subjects as the first day – take the exam in a room where ambient music is playing in the background. If there is a significant difference between the exam scores on the first and second days, then it would be reasonable to conclude that the music had a significant effect on the test subjects' cognitive performance.

❖ One-Way ANOVA

The t-test is designed to handle only two groups at a time. On the other hand, the one-way ANOVA (Analysis of Variance) test can handle three or more groups at a time. Consider an experiment in which we want to determine if there are any significant differences between the cognitive performance of test subjects who are exposed to a variety of musical genres: jazz, rock, classical, and pop. We could either use the same group of test subjects and ask them to take different exams on four different days or, out of practical necessity, we might have four different groups of test subjects take the same math exam in four different classrooms. (We will assume in this experiment that the four groups share a similar aptitude in mathematics.) In each of the classrooms, a different type of music (jazz, rock, classical, and pop) is then played during the exam. After the exam scores are calculated, the one-way ANOVA test can then determine whether there is significant variance among the groups as a whole.

❖ Pearson Correlation

The Pearson correlation coefficient is different from the previous tests in that it seeks to determine not whether there is a significant difference between groups, but whether there is a significant relationship between two different variables. The correlation coefficient (also called *Pearson's r*, the name of the variable) is a value that ranges from -1 to 1. A score of 1 indicates that the two variables have a perfect positive relationship with one another, while a score of -1 indicates the variables have a perfect negative (or inverse) relationship with one another. A score of 0 indicates there is no relationship between the variables.

As another way of thinking about it, a correlation score of 1 means that X and Y increase proportionally with one another. On the other hand, a correlation score of -1 means that as X increases, Y *decreases* proportionally.

We might, for example, create several test subject groups in our "effect of music on cognitive performance" experiment. In this case, we will choose to play the same type of music to each group, but to expose each group to different volume levels. In this case, we might make the hypothesis that as the decibel level of the room increases, the exam results should decrease proportionally. In other words, we are predicting a statistically significant inverse correlation between decibel level and exam score.

To consider an example of positive correlation, we might abandon our music variable and instead examine the correlation between the number of hours that students have slept the night before an exam and their exam score. In this case, we would only need one group. Before the exam, students would be given a survey in which they answer a number of questions about themselves, including how many hours they slept the night before. We might then hypothesize that as the number of sleep hours increases, the exam score will increase proportionally.

5.6 Reading

In this section, you will read an abstract which summarizes a research study. An abstract is very useful because it allows us to get a succinct picture of the basic design and other important aspects of a research study. You will learn more about how to write an abstract in Chapter 10.

The following has been extracted from: Peters, J.C., Polsky, S., Stark, R., Zhaoxing, P., & Hill, J.O. (2014). *Appetite*, *79*, 183-188.

5.6.A

Read the following abstract and discuss answers the questions that follow.

The Influence of Herbs and Spices on Overall Liking of Reduced Fat Food

Abstract

Most adults consume more fat than is recommended in the Dietary Guidelines for Americans. We examined whether adding herbs and spices to reduced-fat foods would improve their consumer liking. We recruited adults 18–65 years old to taste three lunch conditions: full fat (FF), reduced fat with no added spice (RF), and reduced fat plus spice (RFS). Subjects rated their liking of a meatloaf entrée, vegetable side dish, pasta side dish, and overall meal on a 9-point hedonic Likert scale. Subjects came weekly for 3 weeks to consume meals and were randomized to the condition order. We enrolled 148 subjects who were predominantly female (n = 101, 68%), had a mean age of 35.9 years, and body mass index of 24.4 kg/m^2. Subjects reported habitual diets as 36% of total calories from fat (2005 Block Food Frequency Questionnaire). Reducing fat content alone significantly dropped overall liking of the meal compared with FF and RFS conditions (6.29 RF vs. 7.05 FF, $P < 0.0001$; 6.29 RF vs. 6.98 RFS, $P \leq 0.0001$). The RFS overall meal was liked as well as the FF condition. FF and RFS conditions were liked significantly more than RF conditions for each meal item. Liking of FF and RFS meatloaf and vegetables were not significantly different from one another. Pasta FF and RFS conditions were rated significantly differently from each other (7.33 FF vs. 6.61 RFS, $P < 0.0001$). Adding herbs and spices to reduced fat foods restored liking of the overall meal, meatloaf, and vegetables to that of FF conditions, and significantly improved the liking of RF pasta. Herbs and spices can be a useful tool to improve liking of foods consistent with national guidelines.

1. What is the basic problem the researchers were trying to solve with this study? Based on the stated problem, what is the purpose of this study?

2. Based on your response in #1, what is the basic question of this research study?

3. Based on the information in the abstract, what is the null hypothesis in this research study? What is the alternative hypothesis? Write both the null hypothesis and the alternative hypothesis below.

   H_0: ______________________________

   ____

   H_A: ______________________________

   ____

4. How was the research study designed? What were the specific groups in the study that were compared with one another? What is the purpose of creating each of the specific groups?

5. What was the data outcome of the research study? What specific type of evidence was the data outcome? How did the design of the study lead to the data outcome?

6. What conclusion did the researchers make about the original research question and hypotheses? What is the relationship between the data outcome of the study and the conclusion reached by the researchers?

5.7 Writing

5.7.A

After considering all the research design concepts and components in this chapter, brainstorm an idea for your own research project with your partner(s). Answer the following questions in order to develop your research design:

1. What is your central research question?

____

____

____

2. Is your research project an experimental or an observational study?

____

____

3. What are your null and alternative hypotheses?

   H_0: ______________________________

   ____

   H_A: ______________________________

   ____

4. What are your independent and dependent variables?

____

____

____

____

____

5. If your research project is an experimental study, what is the treatment? Does it have any constants?

____

____

____

6. What specific groups are being compared in your study?

7. How do you plan on producing the measurable results of your research study? What specific type of evidence are the results of your research study?

8. How do you plan on making a conclusion about your hypotheses?

Outlining and Writing Your Research Design

- This is the end of Chapter 5. You should now reflect on the research design that will guide your research project for the rest of this course.
- You need to understand the problem or issue your research is trying to answer.
- You need to formulate your basic research question.
- You need to create null and alternative hypotheses which relate directly to your research question.
- You need to consider all the other research design components which have been overviewed in this chapter.

Revision Checklist

Did you ...

- ☐ ask a basic research question which relates directly to a problem or issue that you want to address?
- ☐ write a null and alternative hypothesis for your research project?
- ☐ decide whether your research project is a controlled experiment or an observational study?
- ☐ identify the independent and dependent variables in your study, as well as any constants?
- ☐ identify the specific type of evidence your research project will use?
- ☐ identify the specific groups that are being compared in your study?
- ☐ formulate a plan for reaching a conclusion about the results of your study?

6 Introduction

Explaining key information to introduce your research study

Learning Outcomes:

- to understand the purpose of the introduction section
- to understand the types of information presented in the introduction study
- to understand the differences between various verb tenses
- to learn how to structure your introduction
- to critique an introduction section
- to write your own introduction section with a strong formal style

6.1 Overview

As the big bang is believed by scientists to be the beginning of the universe, the introduction section represents the beginning of your scientific research paper. It introduces your topic by explaining the problem your research is trying to solve and the background information the reader needs to become familiar with your research topic.

All introduction sections of a scientific research paper contain the following types of information:

- key background information and definitions of terms to overview the research topic
- previous research studies to explain what has been completed before your research
- explanations of the purpose and importance of your current research

The background information represents the initial foundation for the explanation of your research, as it helps the reader become sufficiently familiar with your topic and the problem your research study is trying to solve. Overviewing the basic information is important, of course, but it also establishes the importance of your research study. Furthermore, the information on previous research studies demonstrates your understanding and expertise on what has already been accomplished – or not accomplished – in your research topic. In most cases, you will not be the first one to be working on your topic, and it will be both helpful and necessary to establish the specific contribution that your work is making. Finally, explaining the purpose and importance of your research will help readers understand the value of your research and how it will be a solution to the problem.

As we have discussed in the paragraph section of this textbook, writing represents a series of building blocks, with each block dependent on its previously established foundations. A full understanding of the subsequent sections in your paper – methodology, results, and discussion/conclusion – all depends on a clear and thorough introduction.

6.2 Purpose

6.2.A

Consider the following sample introduction, then explain how each sentence relates to a specific type of information from 6.1.

Example: *The first sentence presents the problem and establishes the importance of the enormous waste of energy being used to heat the inside of buildings and suggests that a more efficient insulation method of windows is needed.*

The Insulation Performance of Bubble Wrap Attached to Windows

Introduction

Due to poor window insulation, people have wasted a great deal of energy on indoor heating during the winter. According to the Korea Electric Power Corporation (2017), the electricity usage of Korea has increased 0.5% every year, and winter is one of the peak periods of annual electricity usage. Overuse of energy for heating not only carries a substantial cost, but also damages the environment by burning an increasing amount of fossil fuel. A heated room can maintain its temperature using a small amount of energy if it is well insulated. The most common areas of a house where heat leaks occur are glass windows, window frames, and door frames; therefore, these areas need to be examined to improve insulation efficiency. An insulation sheet, which is a heat retention material used to insulate rooms, can be easily attached to windows to effectively retain heat. This sheet works similarly as a double window – a window with two layers of glass – by forming a layer of air. Originally, bubble wrap was designed to protect fragile objects from being transported, but it has also been proven to work as an effective insulation method.

General methods currently used for indoor insulation include applying Styrofoam to the frames of windows and doors, constructing a double window to create a layer of air between the windows, and installing an air curtain where doors open frequently to stop heat from escaping. Bubble wrap is believed to be the most economical and effective solution, as demonstrated by Lee (2017) in a study that proved bubble wrap attached to windows can increase the room temperature by 2-3 degrees Celsius. The benefits of bubble wrap has lead many people to use it as an insulator today. In spite of this, there have been very few academic studies to examine its efficacy. Although several characteristics of bubble wrap were researched by existing studies, there has been no research about the effect of multilayer cases (Bae, Kang, Choi, & Choi, 2017).

The aim of this study was to find the optimal number of layers which maximizes the performance of bubble wrap insulation. The hypothesis of this experiment was that as the number of bubble wrap layers increases, the performance of the insulation would increase as well. This paper will demonstrate the performance of insulation in correlation with the number of layers of bubble wrap. The results from this study can be applied to real life by helping people use bubble wrap more effectively and reducing the amount of energy used for heating.

6.2.B Discussion and Analysis of the Content and Structure

1. The topic of the research project is clearly explained as the poor insulation of windows. Where do we see the explanation of the need to insulate windows?
2. Where do we see an explanation of bubble wrap?
3. Where do we see an explanation of previous research that has been conducted with bubble wrap?
4. Where is the purpose of the research project explained?

6.3 Language

In the introduction section of your research paper, you may find yourself needing to present information about something that began in the past and was completed, but has a relationship with the present. For these situations, it is necessary to use the present perfect tense. To correctly use the present perfect tense, you must make sure that time is neither specified nor limited because it may be possible that the action occurs again. For example, you cannot use time expressions such as last week, last year, yesterday, a year ago, etc. where the time of the action has been specified and the time is unable to continue. Look at the following examples to get a better understanding.

The microprocessor has malfunctioned twice. ○
The microprocessor has malfunctioned twice since last year. ○
The microprocessor has malfunctioned twice last year. ×
The microprocessor has malfunctioned twice in 2015. ×

In the first example, time is not specified, so the sentence is correct. In the second example, time is mentioned but not specified, and time has not been limited since it only informs us of the starting point: last year. In the third example, time is specified as last year, and the microprocessor is unable to malfunction again in the given time period because last year is over. In the last example, time is specified as 2015, and the microprocessor is unable to malfunction again in 2015 since that year is over.

The present perfect tense is formed by using *has/have + past participle* and making sure time is not specified or limited.

Examples: *The temperature in Seoul* ***has increased*** *for the last 5 years.*
Scientists ***have studied*** *the behavior of gorillas for decades.*
The researchers ***have tested*** *the engines numerous times.*

6.3.A Using Appropriate Grammar

1. In the sample reading from section 6.2, notice the use of the *present perfect* tense in line 1 when the author writes, "...people have wasted a great deal of energy..." Why is the present perfect being used here?

2. Notice the use of the *present perfect passive voice* (refer to 3.4 to review passive voice) grammatical form near the end of the first paragraph when the author writes, "...but it has also been proven to work as an effective insulation method." Why is the present perfect passive voice form being used here? How could we change this statement to the active voice?

3. Notice the use of both the *past passive voice* and *present perfect passive voice* near the end of the second paragraph. As the author writes, "Although several characteristics of bubble wrap *were researched* by existing studies, there *has been* no research about the effect of multilayer cases." Why are the past passive voice and present perfect passive voice forms being used here? What is the difference in meaning between the past passive voice and the present perfect passive voice forms? How could we change this statement to the active voice?

6.4 Goals and Structure

The organization scheme of the introduction section should help the reader to easily and clearly understand your research paper. The following three-paragraph structure can serve as a useful model:

Introduction Section Structure

Opening of the introduction section

- Introduce your topic by presenting an important problem your research is trying to solve
- Provide background information that is informative and supportive of your topic
- Explain any terms necessary to clearly understand your paper
- Present the problem that your research will be focusing on

Body of the introduction section

- Present significant information about previous research on your topic to show what has been completed or how it contributes to your research
- Indicate any weaknesses or gaps found in previous research

Closure of the introduction section

- Explain the purpose of your research
- Present expectations, a hypothesis, or explain how you will conduct your research
- Explain why your research topic is important

Many research papers use more than three paragraphs for their introductions to provide information necessary to help readers understand their topic. The three-paragraph model above is meant to simplify the structure and organization of information to provide a starting point for the research writing process.

6.4.A

Organize the following sentences from 1 to 4 according to the recommended order in the previous section to make a coherent first paragraph for a research paper introduction.

Analyzing the Efficiency of Nitrogen Gas in Packaged Snacks

a. There are many factors that affect the stability of food including humidity, oxygen, physical impact, light, and the time-temperature history of the package. Humidity, for instance, can make dry products lose their desired crispness, and the exposure to oxygen can cause food to spoil. To prevent deterioration of food quality from these factors, Korean snacks are typically packaged in inflated polypropylene bags using nitrogen gas to package them. _____

b. The packaging of snacks is crucial for not only drawing the attention of consumers with an attractive design, but also for preserving the quality of the products. _____

c. In short, gas inflation has been used for the absorption of physical impacts, but the amount of gas used to inflate the bags has caused a dramatic decrease in the amount of food placed per bag. _____

d. Nitrogen gas is a diatomic element which is colorless, odorless, and tasteless. It makes up approximately 78% of the air we breathe, so it is perfect for packaging as a safe means for eating and keeping food fresh. _____

6.4.B

Using the two topics from the previous exercises, try to begin your own introduction by establishing the importance of these topics in one or two sentences.

1. Insulation Performance of Bubble Wrap Attached to Windows

____

____

____

____

2. Analyzing the Efficiency of Nitrogen Gas in Packaged Snacks

Using References and Citations

All research papers should contain references to other publications which provide information that is related to the topic or give further supporting information. The second paragraph of your introduction should demonstrate to the reader that you have done the appropriate research by explaining what questions have been answered regarding your research topic and what questions have not yet been answered. By using citations of previous research papers and other publications, your paper will become more credible and professional.

The most commonly used citation style in the field of engineering, sciences, and social sciences is the APA (American Psychological Association) style. It is important to use citations to avoid plagiarism and give credit to the work of other authors. Furthermore, proper citation allows the reader to easily find the source of information that your paper is referencing.

❖ In-Text Citations

In the humanities, authors will commonly use direct quotes from different sources. However, for engineering, sciences, and social sciences it is more common to summarize or paraphrase from different sources. A summary is a brief explanation of the main points in your own words, while a paraphrase entails a rewrite of the sentence(s) in a similar length to the original in your own words. Any time you use data, facts, or ideas from an outside source in your writing, you must be sure to properly cite your sources.

The following shows the proper structure for citations when paraphrasing or summarizing: Paraphrase/Summary (Author's last name, Year of publication).

Paraphrase/Summary (Author's last name, Year of publication).

Sample:

[9] General methods currently used for indoor insulation include applying Styrofoam to the frames of windows and doors, constructing a double window to create a layer of air between the windows, and installing an air curtain where doors open frequently to stop heat from escaping. [10] Bubble wrap is believed to be the most economical and effective solution, and Lee (2017) indicated that bubble wrap attached to windows can increase the room temperature by 2-3 degrees Celsius. [11] The benefits of bubble wrap has lead many people to use it as an insulator today. [12] In spite of this, there have been very few academic studies to examine its efficacy. [13] Although several characteristics of bubble wrap were researched by existing studies, there has been no research about the effect of multilayer cases (Bae, Kang, Choi, & Choi, 2017).

As you can see in the above sample, in-text citations are used in sentences 10 and 13.

Sentence 10

Bubble wrap is believed to be the most economical and effective solution, and Lee (2017) indicated bubble wrap attached to windows can increase the room temperature by 2-3 degrees Celsius.

In the above extract from the sample, we can see that the citation comes directly after the author's last name, and only the year of the publication is in parentheses because the author's last name is already mentioned in the sentence.

Sentence 13

Although several characteristics of bubble wrap were researched by existing studies, there has been no research about the effect of multilayer cases (Bae, Kang, Choi, & Choi, 2017).

Unlike in sentence 10, the citation in sentence 13 appears in parentheses at the end of the sentence. In sentence 13 though, we also need the authors' last names in addition to the year since the names are not explicitly mentioned in the sentence.

❖ Reference List

In the reference list, the author provides a list of all the sources cited within the text of the research paper. This gives the reader the necessary information to find the source. The sources are all listed in alphabetical order by the author's last name using a specific APA structure depending on the type of source. The following examples represent some of the most common types of sources for the reference section. Note the particular structure in each reference.

Journal Articles Found in Print (one author)

> Author's Last name, F.M. (Year published). Title of article. *Title of Journal, Volume number* (Issue number), pp-pp.

Journal Articles Found Online (two authors)

> First Author's Last name, F.M. & Second Author's Last name, F.M. (Year published). Title of article. *Title of Journal, Volume number* (Issue number), pp-pp. http://dx.doi.org/10.xxxx/xxxxxx

Books Found Online (multiple authors)

> First Author's Last name, F.M., Second Author's Last name, F.M., & Third Author's Last name, F.M. (Year published). *Title of work.* http://dx.doi.org/10.xxxx/xxxxxx

Note: **F** = First name initial **M** = Middle name initial

The following shows a sample of a properly formatted APA reference list. The title should always be 'References' and should be centered. You should also begin your reference list on a new page. You can also notice the use of 'hanging indentations' in the sample below. This means that the first line in each reference stays on the left side of the margin as usual, but any subsequent lines are indented by using the tab key. This is done to make the references visually distinct to readers.

References

Bae, M.J., Kang, J.S., Choi, K.S., & Choi, H.J. (2017). The effect of the attached glazing and windbreak on the thermal performance and air tightness of sliding windows. *KIEAE Journal, 17*(4), 59-65. http://doi.org/10.12813/kieae.2017.17.4.059

Lee, K.M. (2017, December 15). Overuse boiler 'stupid'. Insulation bubble wrap 'great'. *Bulgyo News*. Retrieved from http://www.ibulgyo.com/news/article62633

Maas, S. (2013). The effect of background music on math test performance of high school students. *Journal of Research in Music Education, 54*(4), 293-307.

Seo, J.G. (2015). Evaluation of insulation efficiency of windows and doors according to insulation sheet (bubble wrap) type and location. *Facilities Journal, 44*(11), 72-74.

Zhang, X., Jun, G., & Rhee, K.M. (2016). Comparative evaluation of thermal insulation and solar heat gain in bubble wrap attached window. *Journal of Architectural Institute of Korea, 36*(2), 565-566.

Useful Resource

If you need information on how to structure other types of sources please go to:
https://owl.english.purdue.edu/owl/resource/560/01/
The site map of Purdue OWL has a number of other useful resources that will help you with your academic writing. See pages 148 and 212 for more information on references and citations.

6.4.C

Using the information below, make a reference list using the correct format (everything has been put in lowercase letters for practice purposes).

1. **Title**: music and spatial task performance
   Author: frances h. rauscher, gordon l. shaw, and catherine n. ky
   Journal: nature
   Volume: 365
   Issue: 6447
   Pages: 611
   Year: 1993

2. **Title**: attention drainage effect: how background music effects concentration in taiwanese college students
   Author: peter tze-ming chou
   Journal: journal of the scholarship teaching and learning
   Volume: 10
   Issue: 1
   Pages: 36-46
   Year: 2010

3. **Title**: the effect of background music and noise on the cognitive test performance of introverts and extroverts
   Author: stacey dobbs, adrian furnham, and alastair mcclelland
   Journal: applied cognitive psychology
   Volume: 25
   Issue: 2
   Pages: 307-313
   Year: 2011

References

In the third paragraph of your introduction, you should explain the purpose of your research so that the reader understands the aim of your paper. Use the following formula to clearly express what your research is trying to accomplish.

The aim			this paper			discover		
The goal			this research			determine		
The purpose	+ of +		this experiment	+ is to +		find	+	…
The objective			this test			conclude		
The intent			this investigation			understand		

Example: *The aim of this study is to find the optimal number of layers which maximizes the performance of bubble wrap insulation.*

6.4.D

Change the following statements describing different problems into statements that explain the purpose of testing the problem.

Example: *Students seem to not perform well in class after being deprived of sleep.*
<u>The purpose of this investigation is to discover the effects of sleeping time of students on academic performance.</u>

1. Plants do not seem to grow as well after being watered with only microwaved water.

____

____

2. Ice freezes more quickly when it is made with hot water.

____

____

3. People become more psychologically alert when they exercise regularly.

____

____

4. Water seems to boil faster when salt is added to it.

____

____

5. People who spend too much time on their smartphones appear to have lower attention spans.

____

____

6. Automobile engines perform better in cooler temperatures.

____

____

In addition to expressing your research aims, the third paragraph will also state your *hypothesis*. As explained in Chapter 5, a hypothesis is a prediction or educated guess that can be tested to see whether or not it is correct. A simple method for formulating a hypothesis is to use the *if-then* structure.

Examples: *If the number of bubble wrap layers increases, then the performance of the insulation will increase as well.*
If plants are grown while exposed to classical music, then they will grow larger than plants not exposed to classical music.

6.4.E

Using the statements of purpose that you created in the previous exercise, write a hypothesis explaining your educated guess of the topic.

Example: *The purpose of this investigation is to discover the effects of sleep time of students on academic performance.*
If students increase the amount of time they sleep, then their academic performance will improve.

1. ____

____

2. ____

____

3. ____

____

4. ____

____

5. ____

____

6. ____

____

6.5 Reading

The following has been extracted and adapted from:
Peters, J.C., Polsky, S., Stark, R., Zhaoxing, P., & Hill, J.O. (2014). *Appetite*, *79*, 183-188.

6.5.A

Read the following introduction and examine how each sentence pertains to a part of the introduction section structure introduced in 6.4.

The Influence of Herbs and Spices on Overall Liking of Reduced Fat Food

Introduction

[1] It has proven to be challenging to get people to meet the recommendations provided in the *Dietary Guidelines for Americans*. [2] Consumption of saturated fat is still higher than the recommended 10% of calories (Kachan et al., 2012; Kris-Etherton et al., 2012; US Department of Agriculture & and US Department of Health and Human Services, December, 2010) and total fat intake (of about 33%) is near the upper limit of recommended levels (U.S. Department of Agriculture Center for Nutrition Policy and Promotion Dietary Guidelines for Americans, 2005). [3] Thus, finding ways to reduce fat intake, especially from animal fats, that would be equally palatable to consumers has the potential to improve weight loss efforts among overweight and obese individuals.

[4] Excessive intake of saturated fat is thought to increase risk of coronary heart disease (CHD) (Willett, 2012). [5] Animal fats (like beef, pork, and chicken) are rich in saturated fatty acids (US Department of Agriculture & and US Department of Health and Human Services, December, 2010) and these foods are prevalent in the US diet. [6] A pooled analysis of 11 cohort studies found that substitution of saturated fatty acid intake with polyunsaturated fatty acids is associated with lower incidence of coronary heart disease (Jakobsen et al., 2009). [7] To date, there have been no systematic studies of how effective herbs and spices might be in preserving the liking of food when fat and saturated fat are reduced. [8] This would be the first study of its kind to test this strategy in terms of consumer liking.

[9] This study examined whether addition of herbs and spices to reduced fat and saturated fat foods can improve the overall consumer liking of food consumed at a single

meal occasion. [10] Herbs and spices are among the practical tools available to deliver flavor in a way that is not dependent on fat as the carrier. [11] Our hypothesis was that herbs and spices would offset a significant proportion of the reduction in consumer liking that is typically seen when foods are reduced in fat content. [12] Finding practical and affordable ways for Americans to reduce their total and saturated fat intake without giving up the flavor and enjoyment of food would be a major enabler to help more people meet the guidelines and improve their overall nutrition and health.

Abbreviations: FF, full fat; RF, reduced fat with no added spice; RFS, reduced fat plus spice.

Acknowledgements: Support by the McCormick Science Institute who provided the food for this study. Database support by NIH/NCATS Colorado CTSI Grant Number UL1 TR000154. Contents are the authors' sole responsibility and do not necessarily represent official McCormick Science Institute or NIH views.

Corresponding author. E-mail address: Sarit.Polsky@ucdenver.edu (S. Polsky).

[1] *Present address*: Barbara Davis Center for Childhood Diabetes, Adult Clinic, University of Colorado Denver, Anschutz Medical Campus, 1775 Aurora Court, Room M20-1319, Aurora, CO 80045, USA.

As you can see, the introduction above is organized into three paragraphs. As mentioned on page 123, professional scientific research paper sections will often comprise four paragraphs or more, but the three-paragraph introduction taught in this chapter can serve as a useful model to help you get started. Once you become more comfortable with your writing, you will be able to organize and structure a research paper introduction into as many paragraphs as you see fit.

6.5.B Discussion

1. What problem do the authors present to introduce their paper?
2. What background information do they provide to help the reader understand this topic?
3. What previous research do they present in this introduction?
4. What weakness or gap did they find in this research field?
5. What is the overall purpose of this research paper?
6. What is the hypothesis presented in this paper?
7. What is the purpose of the last sentence?

6.6 Writing

6.6.A

Finish the following introduction section by writing the third paragraph to make a complete introduction. Be sure to include the following information in your writing:

- The purpose of your research
- Expectations, a hypothesis, or an explanation of what you will be testing
- An explanation of why your research topic is important

The Effect of Music Type on the Germination and Development of Kidney Beans

Introduction

As the harmful side effects of chemical fertilizers and pesticides have become more prevalent, people have begun to pay attention to eco-friendly ways of improving plants' growth. One effective eco-friendly method is to use insects to control harmful parasites on plants, such as utilizing *Macroglenes penetrans, parasitic wasps*, to stop *Sitodiplosis mosellana*, wheat midges, from invading wheat (Olfert et al., 2008). In 1989, a Japanese farmer named Furuno invented the "Aigamo method," a special rice farming technique that uses ducks to grow rice. These methods, however, are more financially inefficient than using pesticides because the insects and animals need to be cared for. Therefore, discovering an alternative way that is eco-friendly and does not require a high cost will be a valuable and efficient way to grow plants.

Certain kinds of music help a plant's growth both qualitatively and quantitatively. An Indian botanist named Singh observed that Balsam grew 20% taller and had 72% more leaves after two weeks of playing violin music to the plant, which were much higher than the original average growth rates (Singh, 1955). Another example is the book *The Sound of Music and Plants*, in which Retallack reported that plants leaned towards speakers playing classical music while leaning away from speakers playing rock music (Retallack, 1973). In 1983, the idea became an actual product named "Sonic Bloom," an audio device that helps a plant's growth invented by Dan Carlson (sonicbloom.net). However, previous research studies have mostly focused on the development process of plants rather than the germination process and primarily used western music such as classical music and rock music.

Explanation of research study's purpose

Explanation of research study's hypothesis

Explanation of research study's importance

Outlining and Writing Your Introduction Section

- This is the end of Chapter 6. It is now time for you to think about the introduction section that you will write for your assignment.
- You need to understand the problem your research is trying to answer before you start writing.
- You should be sure to present informative background information so that your reader can become familiar with your topic.
- You need to do research to find information on previous research related to your topic.
- You should define the purpose of your research paper and what your research will be trying to discover.

Revision Checklist

Did you ...

☐ follow the proposed structure for a three-paragraph introduction?

☐ start your introduction by presenting an appropriate problem related to your topic?

☐ provide relevant background information about your topic?

☐ use citations to present information of previous research?

☐ create a reference section to list every source from your citations?

☐ present any weaknesses or gaps found in previous research?

☐ state the purpose of your research using the sentence structure learned in this chapter?

☐ present your educated guess about your experiment by writing a hypothesis or explain how you will conduct your research?

☐ make your topic sound important or valuable?

7 Methodology

Describing the materials, procedures, and data collection methods of your research project

Learning Outcomes:

- to understand the concept of a methodology section
- to explain the rationale of a method
- to learn the language expressions for describing methods
- to understand the goals/organization of a methodology section
- to critique the methodology section of a research paper
- to write a methodology section in a formal academic style

7.1 Overview

The methodology section of your paper requires you to *justify* your choice of research tools by highlighting their strengths and weaknesses.

To further elaborate, you should outline the major *strengths* of your research tools and evaluate their relevance to the main objectives of your study.

The methodology section needs to answer two basic questions about your research project:

- How did you collect or generate the data for your study?
- How did you analyze the data for your study?

As with all scientific writing, you should aim for directness, precision, and clarity in this section. By writing a clear, straightforward account of the step-by-step procedure for your study or research study, the reader should be able to replicate your study. This means that you should explain all the materials, procedures, data collection methods, and data analysis methods in a clear, step-by-step manner.

In short, your aim is to guide the readers of your paper through the process of your study.

7.2 Purpose

When construction of the glass-bottom bridge in the picture below was finished, the following procedures were undertaken to test the strength of the reinforced glass:

- a car full of people was driven across the bridge
- the glass was repeatedly hit with sledgehammers

7.2.A

With your partner(s), discuss the following questions:

1. What do you think the rationale was behind these two tests?
2. Why do you think the car full of people and sledgehammers were chosen as testing methods?
3. How would you describe the procedure of each test?
4. What measurements do you think were made after each test?
5. Would you use the same methods if you were conducting the tests?

7.3 Language

In this section, you are going to learn some common language expressions for methodology writing. We will start with the structures '*to + verb*' and '*in order to + verb*', which are used to explain the rationale of your method/procedures.

'*In order to + verb*' is used when you want to stress the intention of a method that was taken; i.e. your reasoning for taking a certain action.

'*To + verb*', on the other hand, forms the infinitive in the English language. It is not always used to convey intention, but in many cases can be used in place of '*in order to*'. You will need to examine the context to determine the specific usage of '*to + verb*'. Consider the following examples:

1. However, it was imperative for the Skywalk *to open* by the deadline date.
2. Before the actual construction began, every component was measured *to fit* the exact specifications.

Notice how in the first sentence, it would be grammatically incorrect to substitute 'to open' with 'in order to open'. However, in the second sentence, 'in order to fit' could easily replace 'to fit'.

Another issue to consider is when these forms are placed in the beginning of a sentence. Consider the following examples:

3. In order to print something on paper, these components follow a tightly controlled sequence of steps.
4. To elaborate even further, laser printers represent such a substantial improvement on the previous technology that it is difficult to imagine life without them.

While the use of '*in order to + verb*' is preferable in the third sentence, it would be acceptable to replace it with '*to + verb*'. However, it would not be appropriate to substitute '*in order to + verb*' in the fourth sentence. In this case, the writer is seeking to state the purpose of the sentence – it is intended to follow up on the previous sentence with additional details – rather than emphasize the intention of the next clause.

7.3.A

Read the following sentences and decide which form best suits the context of each sentence, or whether either form seems suitable. Explain your decision to your partner.

1. In this research study, two different kites were used *in order to verify / to verify* the functionality of the central wind hole.
2. The test subjects were instructed *in order to complete / to complete* the exam within 30 minutes.
3. *In order to explain / To explain* the procedure, cups of the same material and density were used as the water containers, and 100 ml of distilled water was poured into each sample.
4. When ice covered the surface, the median of the interval was recorded and estimated as the freezing time *in order to reduce / to reduce* a gap from real freezing time.

7.3.B

Complete the following sentences with your own ideas.

1. In order to assess ______________________________.
2. To calculate ______________________________.
3. In order to test ______________________________.
4. To compare ______________________________.
5. In order to estimate ______________________________.
6. To obtain ______________________________.

In Chapter 3 you learned that the *passive voice* is predominantly used when describing processes. Because methodology writing often entails process description, the passive voice is frequently used in this section. However, the *active* voice may occasionally play a role as well.

7.3.C

Explain if the passive or active voice should be used in the following situations.

1. You want to emphasize your decisions, method, or innovation.
2. You want to describe changes made to the conditions of the experiment.
3. You want to describe a result of the experiment.

7.3.D

Explain the different meanings between these sets of sentences:

1. The surface area increased in size. / The surface area was increased in size.
2. The sample size was increased to 20. / The sample size increased to 20.
3. The direction of the wind was changed. / The direction of the wind changed.

It is also important for you to be aware of the different uses of *articles* ('a', 'an', and 'the') when describing your methods as the wrong usage of the article can miscommunicate the context of the procedure that you are aiming to describe. For example, consider how the change in article usage alters the meaning in the two related sentences below:

1. This paper focuses on *the stability* of a kite under different wind conditions.
2. This paper focuses on *a stability* of a kite under different wind conditions.

In #1, the *definite article* 'the' denotes a property of the kite; i.e. its ability to remain stable. Therefore, the definite article usage specifies a unique feature of the kite. In #2, on the other hand, the *indefinite article* 'a' does not actually make it clear that this is a unique property of the kite. The lack of specificity may cause confusion about the exact focus of the paper, as seen below.

3. *The purpose* of the test was to examine the insulation effect of bubble wrap.
4. *A purpose* of the test was to examine the insulation effect of bubble wrap.

In #3, the definite article usage makes it clear that this test had one specific purpose. However, the usage of the indefinite article in #4 implies that the test had other purposes.

7.3.E

Consider the following pairs of sentences. What is the difference between them?

1. The participants then ate a sample. / The participants then ate the sample.
2. An initial temperature was calculated. / The initial temperature was calculated.
3. An amount of soil was added. / The amount of soil was added.

7.3.F

Read the sample paragraph below and fill in the gaps by using *a*, *an*, *the* or, Ø (no article). Be prepared to explain your choices.

This paper focuses on (1. ____) stability of (2. ____) kite under (3. ____) different wind conditions. (4. ____) electric fan was chosen as (5. ____) source of (6. ____) conditions. Additionally, (7. ____) experimenter also assisted by flying (8. ____) kite. During (9. ____) experiment, (10. ____) intensity of (11. ____) wind was fixed at level 3, and (12. ____) direction of (13. ____) wind remained (14. ____) same. Although (15. ____) intensity and (16. ____) direction were fixed, (17. ____) electric fan was considered suitable as (18. ____) wind generated by (19. ____) rotating blades in (20. ____) device is intermittent (Kumon & Ohtsuka, 2013).

Kumon, Y. & Ohtsuka, M. (2013). Development of electric fan propeller featuring chestnut tiger butterfly wing characteristics. *Journal of Aero Aqua Bio-mechanisms, 3*(1), 103-108.

7.3.G

Write eight of your own sentences that include articles and which you plan on using in your methodology section.

After writing your sentences, explain the purpose of each article to your partner(s).

1. ______________________________
2. ______________________________
3. ______________________________
4. ______________________________
5. ______________________________
6. ______________________________
7. ______________________________
8. ______________________________

7.4 Goals and Structure

One of the central aims of the methodology section involves documenting your research transparently. As previously mentioned, explaining the step-by-step procedure of your research means that the reader should be able to replicate your study.

In order to do this, establishing a structural plan is a key step which will function as a template for writing, as well as a way for you to ensure that you are meeting the goals of this section.

The following list outlines the types of general goals you should aim to achieve in this section:

a. Describe previously used methods
b. Describe processes by referring to existing methods in the literature
c. Describe the sample's characteristics
d. Describe background information
e. Provide an overview of the section
f. Provide an overview of the method
g. Explain why a particular method was adopted
h. Explain why a particular method was rejected
i. Explain criteria for selection or inclusion
j. Explain problems or limitations
k. Explain that care was taken
l. Explain the method(s) taken for further analysis

7.4.A

The following sentences provide *example expressions* that achieve the general goals above. Match the expressions and goals by placing the letters **a-l** on the lines below.

1. To verify the growth, a time-lapse camera was used. ___
2. This section explains each stage of the experiment. ___
3. The examination of X, in particular, was complex. ___
4. The process was repeated several times in order to test the design. ___

5. The main drawback of this method was the inconsistency in the results. ___
6. A major advantage of X was its consistent reliability. ___
7. The experiment was divided into three parts labeled 'before', 'during', and 'after'. ___
8. To identify X, the following parameters were used. ___
9. Temperature levels have not commonly been used to analyze data in research of this kind. ___
10. Twenty-one students studying X were recruited for this study. ___
11. The general structure of the experiment was the same as Mpemba's previous test in 1963. ___
12. Various methods have been employed to test glass strength; for example, … ___

As with all academic writing, the methodology section of the research paper itself should have a well-formed structure.

❖ Opening of the methodology section

The opening of the methodology section should explain *how* you designed your experiment and collected the data.

The goals covered in this section might include the following:

- an overview of the section
- an overview of the experiment
- an overview of the objective of the experiment
- a description of the sample's characteristics
- an explanation of the criteria for selection or inclusion

❖ Body of the methodology section

The body could be divided into two separate subsections that explain the following:

1. *Why* you designed your experiment and collected data in this particular manner by covering the following goals:
   - justification for the experiment
   - the purpose of the method
   - description of the processes via references to existing methods in the literature
   - an explanation of why a particular method was adopted / rejected
   - differences in the method from previous research methods

2. How the *experiment progressed* by covering the following goals:
   - the step by step process taken to conduct the experiment
   - an explanation that care was taken

❖ Closure of the methodology section

The closure of the methodology section should explain how you *evaluated* your experiment and data collection processes.

The goals covered in this section might include the following:
   - explaining how the data was collected
   - informing how the data was analyzed
   - showing the method used to validate the data

The sample methodology section below has been written in four separate paragraphs (labeled A–D) to correspond with the three-part structure previously introduced.

Read the paragraph and then answer exercise 7.4.B which follows.

〉**Question:** What are the potential problems with using Wikipedia as a source?

The Effect of Different Types of Music on Kidney Beans' Germination and Development

Methodology

A. 1. This study was conducted to see the effect of music on plant growth. 2. In order to measure the effect of different types of music on kidney beans, 3. the current research study first set up an experiment which played different types of music to 5 different groups of kidney beans, then measured and analyzed the changes observed in each group.

B. 4. The current research study investigated music's effect on kidney beans since they are relatively less sensitive to their environment and grow faster than other kinds of beans; therefore, they allow observation both on germination and development. In fact, kidney beans are often used in biology experiments for these reasons (Wikipedia). 5. The experiment was designed based on the research of Chivukula and Ramaswamy (2014) which successfully showed that classical music had positive effects, while rock music had negative effects on the growth of *rosa chinensis* (Chinese roses) **6.** In comparison with their study, the only changes in the current research study were the samples used in the experiment and the addition of Korean traditional music as a variable.

C. **7.** The experiment proceeded as follows; first, a total of 40 kidney beans were divided into 5 groups of 8, including one control group and four groups exposed to music. **8.** Then, the beans were kept inside a room where no sunlight was present as they prefer a cooler environment between 13 and 18 °C (Wikipedia). **9.** All the groups were supplied with an equal amount of water through 2 sheets of soaked cotton placed under them and a sheet of soaked tissue placed above the beans in order to minimize the differences aroused from variation in the water supply. **10.** Following this, the sheets of cotton and the tissue were soaked every day. **11.** The 4 different kinds of music used in the experiment were as follows: classical – "Claire De Lune," by Debussy, heavy metal – "The Beautiful People," by Marilyn Manson, Korean traditional music – "Jongmyo Shrine Music," and contemporary music – "Klangstudie II," by Herbert Eimert. **12.** The music was played to each group for 30 minutes a day through a speaker of the same volume level. **13.** In order to obtain quantitative analysis of the effect of music on the kidney beans, the following factors were selected to digitize the growth of the beans: the number of sprouts from the germination process, the width and number of the leaves, and the height and length of the internode of the plant 18 days after the development process.

D. **14.** Although biological differences between the beans – such as inborn nutritive conditions – was a control variable, it was impossible to completely eliminate the difference. **15.** However, the beans were randomly separated; hence, the average tendency of each group observed was still considered to be valid.

Chivukula, V. & Ramaswamy, S. (2014). Effect of different types of music on Rosa chinensis plants. *International Journal of Environmental Science and Development*, *5*(5), 431.

Kidney bean. (n.d.). In Wikipedia. Retrieved May 14, 2017, from https://en.wikipedia.org/wiki/Kidney_bean

7.4.B

Revisit the previously outlined structure, and with your partner(s) *explain the goals* of each of the numbered sections.

1. ______________________________
2. ______________________________
3. ______________________________
4. ______________________________
5. ______________________________
6. ______________________________
7. ______________________________
8. ______________________________
9. ______________________________
10. ______________________________
11. ______________________________
12. ______________________________
13. ______________________________
14. ______________________________
15. ______________________________

Some students may wish to understand the essence of each paragraph in the above sample.

7.4.C

Brainstorm the key function of each paragraph in sections A-D of the above sample with your partner(s).

a. ______________ b. ______________

c. ______________ d. ______________

In the excerpt above, you will notice certain language expression which serve a specific purpose. For instance, the following excerpts justify certain actions in the experiment:

'In order to measure the effect of different types of music on kidney beans, ...'

'... since they are relatively less sensitive to their environment and grow faster ...'

'... as they prefer a cooler environment between 13 and 18 °C.'

'... in order to minimize the differences aroused from variation in the water supply.'

'In order to obtain quantitative analysis of the effect of music on the kidney beans, ...'

As you can see, the methodology section should include *specific language goals*, which may in turn include the following *additional language goals*:

a. Describing the process with verbs in the passive form
b. Describing the process with infinitive of purpose
c. Describing the process with sequence words and phrases
d. Describing the process with adverbs of manner
e. Describing the process with 'using' + instrument

7.4.D

The following sentences provide *example expressions* that achieve the *language goals* above.
Match the expressions and goals by placing the letters **a-e** on the lines below.

1. The entire analysis was conducted by using Excel. ____
2. The mold was gently pressed to see if it would reform. ____
3. When dividing X, care was taken to maintain the same levels. ____
4. Data were collected on two occasions. ____
5. The final stage of the experiment was to ... ____

Evaluating Reference Materials

The methodology section of the kidney beans experiment (see 7.4.A) uses Wikipedia as a source, which actually represents a flaw in the writing that should be fixed. Formal academic writing should avoid using Wikipedia as a source because it is a blog that anyone can edit. This also applies to other public platforms that people can freely edit.

This does not mean that all other non-editable platforms are suitable to use as they may not meet other important criteria. The following framework provides criteria that can help determine the suitability of a source that you intend to use.

Credibility	Is the author of the reference an authority (expert) in the specific field? This is important as it can help you to determine whether the author's assertions are credible.
Intent	What is the intention of the research? This can be useful in determining the purpose for including the information. For instance, there may be emotional language or evidence of bias based on the omission of facts or data.
Timeliness	Over time, some research may be compromised by more recent research. It is therefore necessary for you to make sure that what you use has not become dated.
Exactness	It is important for you to ensure that the information you use is accurate. Errors can lead to faulty reasoning and also damage your own credibility.
Information	How is the information pertinent to your research? This is important as the references you cite need to support your ideas by being relevant.
Take/Toss?	If you are satisfied that the reference meets the above criteria, take it by writing it as an APA citation and reference. If not, toss it aside and find something more suitable.

C.I.T.E. I.T.

An effective way to remember the above framework criteria is the acronym C.I.T.E. I.T.
If the reference satisfies all elements of the C.I.T.E. I.T. framework, then WRITE IT!

When searching for references, it is advisable to use https://scholar.google.co.uk/
This will provide you with research papers from published peer-reviewed journals. Moreover, if you want to use a paper from Google Scholar you can click this icon **”**, which will provide you with the formatted APA citation you will need for your reference list.

Some articles (e.g. newspaper or magazine articles) will not be in the Google Scholar database. In this case, you will need to write this citation manually.
The following online tool can help you with this task: http://www.citationmachine.net/

As a researcher you will need to effectively manage your references. The website https://www.zotero.org/ is a free, open-source research tool used by experienced academic researchers, and is highly recommended.

7.5 Reading

The methodology section below has been extracted and adapted from the following paper: Peters, J.C., Polsky, S., Stark, R., Zhaoxing, P., & Hill, J.O. (2014). *Appetite*, *79*, 183-188.

Read the research paper excerpt and discuss the questions that follow in 7.5.A.

The Influence of Herbs and Spices on Overall Liking of Reduced Fat Food

Experimental Design

[1] This study tested the overall consumer acceptability of three different lunch conditions using a randomized, three-period, within subjects, crossover design. [2] The three test conditions were (1) full fat (FF), (2) reduced fat (and calorie) with no added spice (RF), and (3) reduced fat (and calorie) plus spice (RFS). [3] The two reduced fat meals were matched for calories. [4] The test meals were composed of meatloaf with gravy, mixed vegetables (broccoli and cauliflower), and creamy pasta (penne). [5] Subjects were blinded to the test meal conditions. [6] Adults aged 18–65 were recruited from the University of Colorado Anschutz Medical Campus and surrounding community using campus announcements and online postings. [7] Prospective subjects were screened by phone or by completing a brief survey. [8] Qualified subjects were asked to sign an informed consent. [9] Some subjects were excluded because they were diagnosed with sensory disorders and allergies to the test food, and inability to complete the protocol.

Experimental Procedure

[10] There were limited previous data for estimating the potential effect size for this study. [11] Based on the study of liking of soup by Essed, Kleikers, van Staveren, Kok, and de Graaf (2009) where a 10 point Likert scale was used, data was collected from 120 subjects in this experiment. [12] Subjects were individually randomized into blocks of six participants, each with a different treatment sequence, representing all the possible order combinations of the three test conditions (FF, RF, and RFS). [13] As such, equal distributions of the number of test conditions and of treatment sequences was accomplished if the number of participations was a multiple of six. [14] A random list of 120 participants was generated using SAS procedure, Proc Plan. [15] Prior to testing, subjects completed an electronic 110-item 2005 Block Food Frequency Questionnaire (FFQ) (Block,

Woods, Potosky, & Clifford, 1990; Subar et al., 2001) to estimate habitual fat and saturated fat intake as a percentage of total calories consumed over the previous year.

[16] All three test meals comprised the same items: meatloaf with gravy, broccoli and cauliflower in butter sauce, and penne with creamy white sauce. [17] The three types of food were as follows: the full fat version of meatloaf and creamy pasta in a white sauce containing cream (whipping cream and half and half cream) and cheese, the reduced fat meatloaf and the creamy pasta sauce made with milk instead of cream, and the reduced fat with herbs and spice version used the same ingredients as the RF version but with additional herbs and spices. [18] Subjects were served three meals between 11 and 1 PM on the same day of the week and the same hour of the day for each of the three test meals. [19] Subjects were given 30 minutes to consume the meal and complete the evaluation questionnaire. [20] The weight of food consumed was collected as an indicator for how liking affected the amount of food consumed.

Statistical Analysis

[21] Subjects completed a 9-point Likert scale questionnaire that assessed their liking. [22] The scales were anchored by "dislike extremely" to "like extremely" at the two ends. [23] The demographic characteristics and dietary habits of subjects were tabulated using summary statistics. [24] T-tests and chi-squared tests were used to compare characteristics and dietary habits between subjects to examine whether any significant differences were present among different groups of subjects.

References

Block, G., Woods, M., Potosky, A., & Clifford, C. (1990). Validation of a self-administered diet history questionnaire using multiple diet records. *Journal of Clinical Epidemiology, 43*(12), 1327–1335.

Essed, N.H., Kleikers, S., van Staveren, W.A., Kok, F.J., & de Graaf, C. (2009). No effect on intake and liking of soup enhanced with mono-sodium glutamate and celery powder among elderly people with olfactory and/or gustatory loss. *International Journal of Food Sciences and Nutrition, 60*(Suppl. 5), 143–154. doi:10.1080/ 09637480802710216. [Clinical Trial Controlled Clinical Trial Research Support, Non-U.S. Gov't].

Subar, A.F., Thompson, F.E., Kipnis, V., Midthune, D., Hurwitz, P., McNutt, S., et al. (2001). Comparative validation of the Block, Willett, and National Cancer Institute food frequency questionnaires: The Eating at America's Table Study. *American Journal of Epidemiology, 154*(12), 1089–1099. [Clinical Trial Comparative Study Randomized Controlled Trial Validation Studies].

Note: Before reflecting on the questions in 7.5.A, read the following notes which explain the purpose of certain sections of the research paper. The sections which the notes are referring to have been underlined in the paper excerpt for ease of reference.

The following defines some of the terminology that is used in this section:

- *Likert scale* – refers to a specific type of survey question where the scale usually ranges from "strongly" agree to "strongly disagree."

In the first section, which is entitled Experimental Design, the following sentence appears:

"Subjects were blinded to the test meal conditions."

This is referring to a blind experiment, an experiment in which information is hidden from the test subjects until after the experiment has been performed.

Additionally, in the first section the following clause appears:

"Adults aged 18-65 were recruited from the University of Colorado Anschutz Medical Campus and surrounding community..."

Since human beings were an essential part of this experiment, it is natural to explain where the test subjects came from. The source of the food does not appear to be explained in this paper.

7.5.A

After reading the methodology section excerpt above, discuss the following questions.

1. What is the purpose of the first section, which is entitled Experimental Design?
2. How do the procedures presented in the sections entitled Experimental Procedure relate to the methodology as a whole?
3. A sentence in the section entitled Experimental Procedure states as follows:

   "Subjects were individually randomized into blocks of six participants, each with a different treatment sequence, representing all the possible order combinations of the three test conditions (FF, RF, and RFS)."

   What problems do you think might occur in this experiment if a non-randomized group had been used?
4. In the section entitled Experimental Procedure, highlight the language phrases which explain the reason for taking a certain action.

5. In the final Statistical Analysis section, the following phrase appears:
   "... to examine whether any significant differences were present among different groups of subjects."
   Explain why "significant differences" could indicate that the results were biased.
6. Using the *goals and structure* of the methodology section overviewed in 7.4, *summarize the goals* of each section below by *highlighting the language phrases* that are used to achieve each goal.

A. Experimental Design

B. Experimental Procedure

C. Statistical Analysis

7.6 Writing

Read the methodology section below. After you finish, turn to exercise 7.6.A and match the missing information by placing a letter to a corresponding number.

Analyzing the Efficiency of Nitrogen Gas in Packaged Snacks

Methodology

The current study involved selecting three major confectionery companies in South Korea: Lotte, Orion, and Haitai. These brands were investigated because they are the top three confectionery companies in sales, and [**1.** ____] according to the Financial Supervisory Service's investigation in 2015.

The study did not measure the volume share of the products' content; instead, [**2.** ____]. Measuring the volume share was regarded to be implausible in this study [**3.** ____]. Meanwhile, the kind of snack products remained constant as 'potato chips' for each brand [**4.** ____]; for instance, popcorn has a much lower density than crackers, which means the volume of popcorn is larger than crackers even if they have identical weight. [**5.** ____], the contents' density had to remain the same between each brand.

Potato chips are one of a few kinds of snack that are produced from all three companies, which is an appropriate snack to choose to make objective comparisons between each company. The flavor was also controlled as 'salty' [**6.** ____], which could lead to different quantity of contents. [**7.** ____]: Lay's from Lotte, Poca Chips from Orion, and Seng Seng Chips from Haitai.

More than one sample was needed for each brand [**8.** ____]. Therefore, 5 samples were collected for each product and then analyzed for the ratio of weight to volume. [**9.** ____], and the volume was estimated by sinking the unopened products into a bowl full of water [**10.** ____]. Measuring volume took priority over weight measurement in sequence [**11.** ____], leaving the polypropylene bag and nitrogen out. Finally, the mean of the weight to volume ratios for each brand was compared [**12.** ____]. A statistical method called "One-way Analysis of Variance (One-way ANOVA)" was used [**13.** ____].

7.6.A

Match the following lettered phrases to the numbers 1-13 in the above methodology section.

a. to verify that the differences of each mean are statistically significant
b. the market share of the three companies is estimated at about 60%
c. because comparing ratios of weight to volume in different snack types was considered illogical
d. to eliminate the possibility of selecting defective products
e. An electronic scale was used to weigh the snacks
f. and measuring the volume of overflowed water
g. because potato chips with a different flavor would have a notable difference in ingredient costs
h. because the snacks had to be opened to exclusively weigh the contents
i. to determine whether the null hypothesis was rejected or not
j. In order to consider the ratio of weight to volume equivalent to the volume share of a product's content
k. As a result, the selected products from each confectionery company are as follows
l. a ratio of weight to volume was gauged for each product
m. because excluding minute gaps between each piece of snack while taking the contents' volume was impossible

Read the following sample of a methodology section explaining how the insulation performance of bubble wrap was tested.

The Insulation Performance of Bubble Wrap Attached to Windows

Methodology

This study was performed in November 2018 in an indoor environment. The purpose of the test was to determine the insulation effect of bubble wrap attached to a window. A crucial variable of the experiment was the terminal temperature (also called equilibrium temperature), which is the temperature of an object when the thermal conduction is in a steady state condition. By measuring the terminal temperature of the constant-powered object, the thermal conductivity of the object, which represents how well a given material delivers heat, can be found via a relatively straightforward equation. Zhang, Jun, and Rhee (2016) proposed that the standard method of measuring indoor insulation effect should measure both thermal conductivity and light transmittance, a term related to sunlight exposure. Due to a lack of equipment, however, only thermal conductivity was measured in this experiment.

A 40 cm sized cubic box made with Styrofoam boards was considered a model for a house. One of the side faces of the box was opened and then used as a position of the window, and an acrylic board with 0.5 cm thickness was used as the window. Based on the assumption that heat only escapes at the window, Styrofoam (a strong insulation material) was used. A 220 V-30 W light bulb was installed in order to apply heat, and a temperature sensor was placed in the box at a distance of 15 cm to avoid any direct effect from the bulb. Bubble wrap with a bubble radius of 0.5 cm was then attached to the window and installed to face the inside of the box. The size and thickness of all bubble wrap sheets were kept constant, and the numbers of layers varied from one to five. A bare acrylic board without bubble wrap served as the control group for this test.

The experiment was conducted as follows: First, the air in the box was ventilated, and the room temperature was then measured. Next, the window with bubble wrap attached to it was carefully taped on the opened side of the box. After the box was ready, the light bulb was turned on. From this point onwards, the temperature of the box was checked consistently to see when the box reached its terminal temperature. Once the box temperature stabilized, it meant that it had reached its terminal temperature. In this experiment, the box reached its terminal temperature after approximately 50 minutes. Finally, the terminal temperature was recorded. The control group and layer groups (from one to five) were then tested, and the terminal temperature measurement was repeated seven times in three-minute intervals.

Reaching the terminal temperature meant that the power of the light bulb and thermal energy loss rate of the box were the same. To prevent heat from escaping, the holes in the bulb wire and sensor wire were sealed tightly. The thermal conductivities of the various layers of bubble wrap were then calculated.

7.6.B

Soundproofing experiments test different materials to see which is the best at soundproofing. They may have some similarities to the experiment on bubble wrap insulation performance described above. Search online for a video demonstrating a soundproofing experiment. Re-read the methodology section of the bubble wrap experiment described above then, using a similar structure, write the method used in the soundproofing experiment you viewed in the space below.

The opening of the methodology section

The body of the methodology section

The closure of the methodology section

Outlining and Writing Your Methodology Section

- This is the end of Chapter 7. It is now time for you to think about the methodology section that you will write for your assignment.
- Before you start drafting, you should go through the pre-writing process and create a clear outline that shows the coherence (logical connection) of each part of the stages in the methodology you are writing about.
- You should write this section of your research paper in four sections, although it does not necessarily mean that it will equal 4 paragraphs.
- It is not a requirement for you use subtitles for each section, but they can make the flow of the sections easier for the readers to follow.
- After you have created your rough draft, use the revision checklist below to make editorial changes.

Revision Checklist

Did you ...

- ☐ write in the past tense when describing the procedures taken?
- ☐ use the active and passive voice where appropriate?
- ☐ provide enough information so that your experiment could be replicated?
- ☐ explain the rationale for choosing your methods?
- ☐ ensure that you use the correct article (a, an, the) for a specific purpose?
- ☐ explain your criteria for choosing any special materials/equipment or unusual methods that differ from commonly accepted procedures?
- ☐ explain how data was collected?
- ☐ explain in simple terms any complex statistical methods that you are using?
- ☐ use the C.I.T.E. I.T. framework to evaluate your reference materials?

8 Results

Writing about the outcome of your experiment

Learning Outcomes:

- to understand the purpose of writing the results section
- to learn the structural components of the results section
- to understand specific language features of the results section
- to learn how to present your results using visual representations such as tables and graphs
- to learn how to present your results using different types of statistical analysis

8.1 Overview

The results section is by far the most data-intensive segment in a scientific research paper. It also, along with the methodology section, has the least text in the research paper. Its brevity should not undermine its importance, though, as the data obtained from your research study represents the evidential foundation for analyzing your research, answering your original research question(s), and achieving the ultimate aim(s) of your study.

In the results section, the key findings of the research study should be reported in the form of data amassed through the research. This can include findings which support your original hypothesis, findings which refute it, or findings which are completely unexpected, or even unwanted. A summary of statistical analyses of the data should also be included in this section.

The research study's outcome(s) should be reported in two forms: the written form in the main body of the text, and the non-textual form via components such as tables, graphs, and other types of illustrations. Visualization of the data can help readers understand the findings of the research more effectively and intuitively.

Information in the results section should be entirely objective and therefore unbiased. Further interpretation of the data is unnecessary and rarely delivered in the results section; the interpretation of the results should be saved for the discussion/conclusion section. One grammatical point to note is that the results section is primarily written in the past tense, as you are reporting findings from research that is already complete. The only case when the present tense should be used is when referring to the information presented in the illustrations. As with all scientific writing, this section should prioritize directness, precision, and clarity. In short, your aim is to guide the readers of your paper through the findings of your research study in a clear and easy-to-understand manner.

8.2 Purpose

The main goal of the results section is to objectively present the key results of the experiment without any subjective interpretation. The presentation of information in this section serves as the basis for ultimately reaching the conclusion(s) in your study, and hence marks a clear and crucial transition into the final phase of your paper.

As a starting point for understanding this section, examine the following pictures that summarize a simple experiment about the moving distance depending on liquid viscosity.

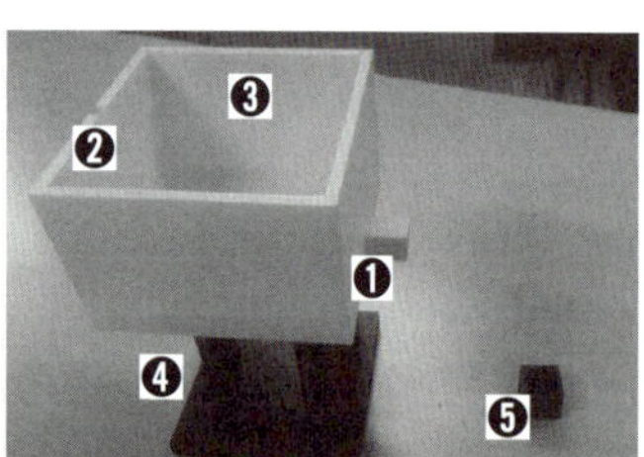

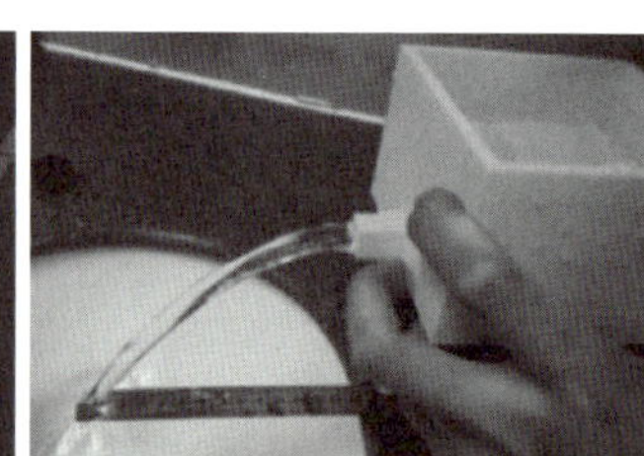

8.2.A

With your partner(s), discuss the following questions:

1. What is the topic and the research question of this experiment?
2. What is the procedure of the experiment? How would you describe it?
3. What are the results of the experiment?
4. What would you do differently if you were conducting this experiment?
5. Do you have any suggestions for improving the procedure?

8.3 Goals and Structure

In the results section, your primary aim is to convey the key results of your research to the readers in a clear and precise manner, as the readers cannot be expected to fully understand the research study you conducted. In order to do this, establishing a structural plan of the results section is a key step that will function as a template for writing as well as a guidance tool for reading.

❖ Opening of the results section

The opening of the results section should strive to achieve two main goals: to create a smooth transition from previous sections and to effectively open the results section. You have two distinct ways to write this section:

1. Review some part(s) of the previous section(s). You, as the author of the paper, should not expect the readers to remember what you have said in the previous sections. Thus, you should consider reviewing the following ideas:
   - the main goal of your research study
   - the research question(s)
   - the hypotheses to be tested
   - the methodology
   - the findings from other previous research that can directly relate to your findings
2. Preview the results section by providing general statements about the key findings. This will direct the readers to interpret the results as you, the author, originally intended.
   - the overview of the key results
   - the overview of the statistical analyses
   - the general pattern(s) of the key results
   - any information that may help the readers understand the results section; e.g., the reason why some participants' data were excluded from data analysis

❖ Body of the results section

In the body, the key results are presented in the text as well as in any figures and tables.

3. Describe the key findings in the text with the aid of tables, graphs, and other illustrations. It is important to evaluate and delineate your results since not all the results are necessarily relevant to the aims of the research study, nor are they

particularly interesting to the reader. The tables, graphs, and other images should be carefully constructed so that the information in the illustrations is consistent with the main body of the text. The results from statistical analyses should be reported in detail, often with a table (or tables) comprising descriptive and inferential statistics.

4. Compare the results of the current research study with previous research. It is important to make the readers understand whether, where, and how your findings are in corroboration (or discord) with the findings of the previous research studies.

❖ Closure of the results section

The results section can be completed by presenting some unwanted results and/or interpretations of important results.

5. Describe some important but unwanted results. Any problems or limitations in your study should be neither hidden nor disregarded. However, you may choose to minimize the significance of the problems and limitations, or to offer potential solution(s). Acknowledging the problems and limitations of your research study does not devalue your research; rather, it strengthens its credibility.
6. Discuss implications, contributions, and/or applications of your research. This will be primarily covered in the discussion/conclusion section; however, you do not need to wait until the discussion/conclusion section in order to provide a brief discussion of the meaning of your research. You can select elements to preview in the results section in order to ensure the better flow of writing and give the readers some indication of the meaning of your research study.

8.3.A

Read the following excerpts from the results section of various research papers.
Match each excerpt to the aims above by writing # 1-6 on the provided lines.

a. As mentioned earlier, the main goal of the experiment was to see if there is any difference between the average GPA of freshmen and seniors. ___
b. The present study examined the effect of altitude on temperature change using the simulation program. ___
c. The average GPA of the senior students was 15% higher than the freshmen's. ___
d. The results were somewhat inconsistent with the findings from Kim (2016). ___

e. Although the results were not statistically significant, differences across groups were consistent with the hypotheses. ___
f. The speed of wind exceeded 156 km/h in the wind tunnel but then dramatically decreased. ___
g. The resulting patterns of plant growth were very similar to those observed by Cole and Mo (2017). ___
h. As can be seen in Fig. 3, wind speed eventually leveled off at 100 km/h. ___
i. The ANOVA analysis showed that the mean differences among all age groups were statistically significant ($F = 6.87$, $p < .001$). ___
j. To identify the physiological effect of stress, the present research study measured the blood pressure and heart beat rate of 30 college students ranging from 20 to 25 years old. ___
k. A paired t-test between pre- and post-test revealed that mental training influenced the test takers positively. ___

The following has been extracted and adapted from:
Wells, D.L., Coleman, D., & Challis, M.G. (2006). *Applied Animal Behaviour Science, 100*, 327-332.

8.3.B.1

Read the following sample results section and place numbers 1-4 on the lines below in a-f to explain the purpose they serve in the coherence of describing the results.

1. There was no significant effect of auditory stimulation on any of the gorillas' behaviors ($p > 0.05$ for all Friedman ANOVAs). 2. However, the animals tended to spend more of their time resting and sitting during the ecologically relevant, and in particular the ecologically non-relevant, conditions of auditory stimulation than the control group (Table 2). 3. Compared to the control group, the ecologically relevant, and in particular the ecologically non-relevant, condition encouraged more social interactions and less moving, standing, and autogrooming. 4. Importantly, aggressive behaviors were reduced by more than 50% and abnormal behaviors by more than 30% in the ecologically non-relevant condition compared to the control group (Table 2).

Table 2. Gorillas' behaviors per condition of auditory stimulation.

Behavior	Control group mean (S.E.)	Ecologically relevant mean (S.E.)	Ecologically non-relevant mean (S.E.)	P
Resting	89.7 (26.0)	99.3 (23.9)	100.7 (30.7)	0.73
Standing	21.7 (3.2)	17.7 (3.1)	15.0 (3.5)	0.07
Sitting	176.3 (35.8)	201.3 (36.5)	202.7 (33.7)	0.07
Moving	16.3 (3.7)	12.7 (2.4)	12.0 (4.0)	0.11
Aggression	5.3 (3.2)	4.3 (2.8)	2.3 (1.7)	0.09
Social	11.0 (4.8)	12.3 (6.6)	13.7 (6.5)	0.82
Abnormal	18.7 (11.8)	14.3 (10.4)	12.0 (10.1)	0.07
Autogroom	27.3 (7.2)	22.0 (5.9)	20.7 (6.1)	0.40

Note: The mean±S.E. number of times gorillas were recorded exhibiting each behavior during the three conditions of auditory stimulation. P-values arising from Friedman ANOVAs are presented.

a. Review certain part(s) of the previous section(s). ____________

b. Preview the results section by providing general statements about the key findings. ____________

c. Describe the key findings in the text, often with the aid of tables, graphs, and other images. ____________

d. Compare the results of the current research study with those of previous research studies. ____________

e. Describe important but unwanted results. ____________

f. Discuss implications, contributions, and/or applications of your research. ____________

8.3.B.2

Read the sample results section of a student's research paper and place numbers 1-4 on the lines below in a-f on page 166 to explain the purpose they serve in the coherence of describing the results.

1. Water samples from three sites (the source and the inlet and outlet of Jahayeon pond) were collected. The discoloration of the filtering paper and the weight of the residue were measured in order to compare water quality. 2. Fig. 1 shows the images of the dried filter papers used to filter 4 different water

samples: water samples from the inlet, outlet, and source of Jahayeon, as well as a control sample of distilled water. 3. As seen in Fig. 1, there was no observable color difference between the filter paper used for the source of Jahayeon and the one for the distilled water. 4. However, both filter papers used for the inlet and outlet of Jahayeon were contaminated with dirt, which subsequently discolored the paper.

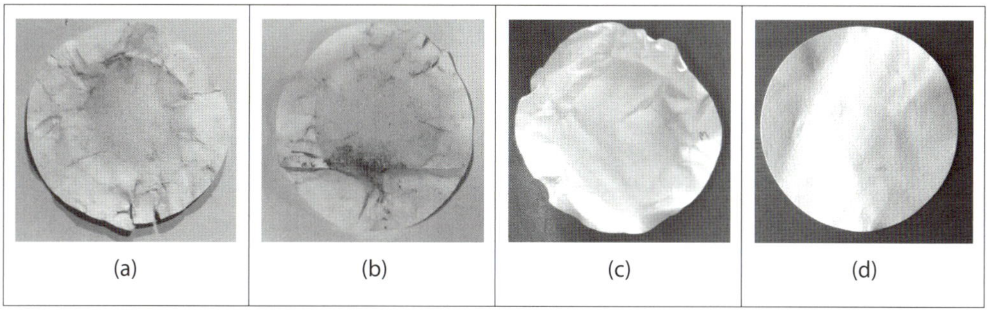

Figure 1. The photos of the dried filter papers used to filter the water from three different sampling sites (a, the inlet of Jahayeon; b, the outlet of Jahayeon; c, the source of Jahayeon) and the distilled water (d, control group).

5. Fig. 2 exhibits the weights of the residue measured from the three sites after filtering the samples and drying the filter paper. 6. As expected, the weights of the residue collected from the inlet and outlet of Jahayeon were much greater than that of the source. 7. However, the mean difference observed between the weight of the inlet and outlet of Jahayeon was minimal.

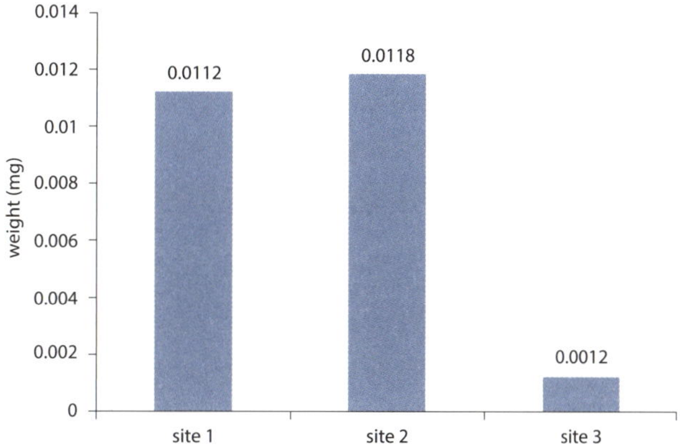

Figure 2. The mean weight (mg) of the residue measured from three sites: site 1, Jahayeon inlet; site 2, Jahayeon outlet; site 3, Jahayeon source. The weight of the residue was calculated by subtracting the weight (mg) of the filter paper after filtering the distilled water and drying it from the weight (mg) of the filter paper after filtering the water from each site and then drying it.

8. The findings regarding the combined discoloration and weight difference suggest the water in Jahayeon has been contaminated by students' misconduct such as littering. 9. However, in order to fully understand and evaluate the water quality of Jahayeon, further statistical analyses and investigation on the composition of the residue is necessary.

a. Review certain part(s) of the previous section(s). ______________

b. Preview the results section by providing general statements about the key findings. ______________

c. Describe the key findings in the text, preferably with the aid of tables, graphs, and other images. ______________

d. Compare the results of the current research study with those of previous research studies. ______________

e. Describe important but unwanted results. ______________

f. Discuss implications, contributions, and/or applications of your research. ______________

8.3.B.3

Read the results section again and discuss the following questions.

1. Are all the sentences consistently written in a single verb tense?
   If yes, what tense is it?
   If not, what other tense(s) is/are used?

2. Are the results objectively reported?
   If not, identify the specific issue(s) that you see, and explain how you would modify the language to be more objective.

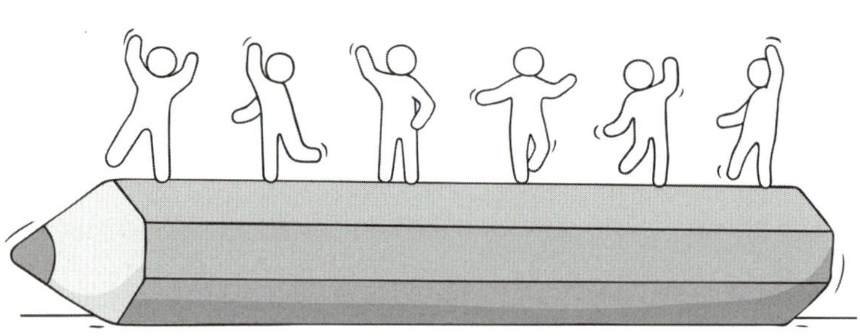

8.4 Illustrations

As discussed in the previous section, the results section employs many different types of illustrations. The illustrations must contain all the information which is necessary to understand the results. Illustrations are considered the best way to communicate information to the readers, especially in science and engineering fields. Therefore, constructing clear, self-explanatory illustrations is arguably even more important than presenting the same information in the text.

When reporting the results in the form of illustrations, it is important to be aware of the following issues:

1. The visual materials should facilitate transparent communication with the reader. The illustrations should not be used solely for aesthetic purposes. Moreover, the information of the illustrations should not mislead the readers in any way.

2. Among the many different types of illustrations, the most appropriate form should be carefully chosen. Furthermore, the same data should not be presented in multiple forms of illustrations.

3. All the illustrations should be clear, concise, and self-explanatory. Each illustration must have a caption where its title and more detailed information, if necessary, are presented. Without reference to the text but with the carefully constructed caption, the reader should be able to understand the information presented in the illustrations.

4. All the visual materials included in the paper must be discussed in the body of the text. No illustration should be left without any explanation. However, instead of simply listing all the information included in the illustration, the text should guide the reader to focus on the important information.

5. Tables and figures should be separately numbered. For example, the third table in your paper will be numbered as Table 3, the third figure as Fig. 3, and so on and so forth.

8.4.A

Look at the following illustrations. With your partner(s), state the name for each type of illustration, and what type of data is appropriate for it.

A.

Table 1

An example table with headings.

Heading 1	Heading 2	Heading 3
Group 1	123	234
Group 2	456	567
Group 3	789	891
Totals (*N* = 3060)	1368	1692

B.

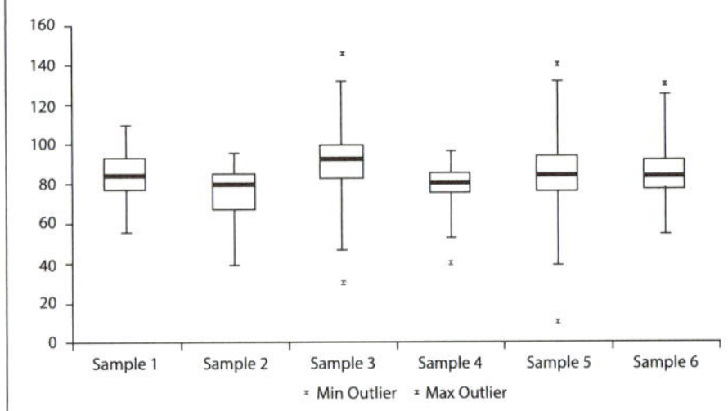

Figure 1. An example box and whisker plot from the Box Plot Template showing the IQR, whiskers, and max/min outliers.

C.

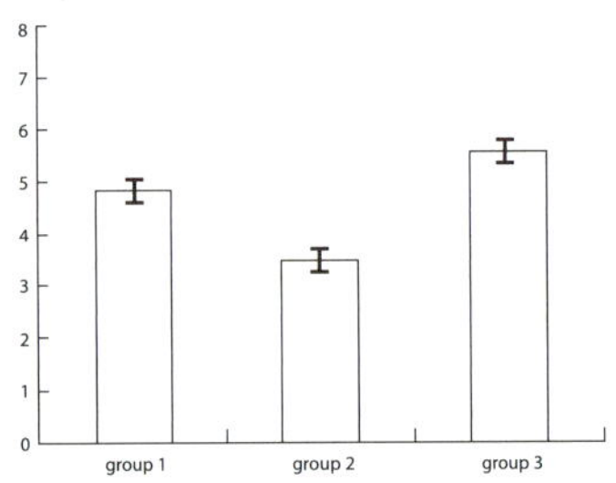

Figure 2. An example bar graph with error bars. Error bars represent standard errors.

D.

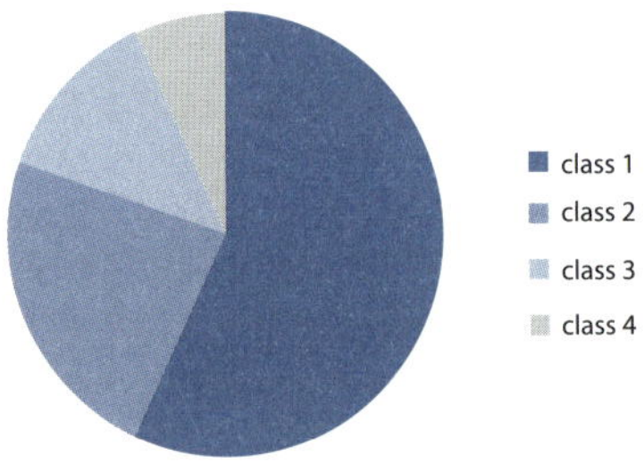

Figure 3. An example pie chart. The slices in the pie chart are generally arranged from the largest to the smallest.

E.

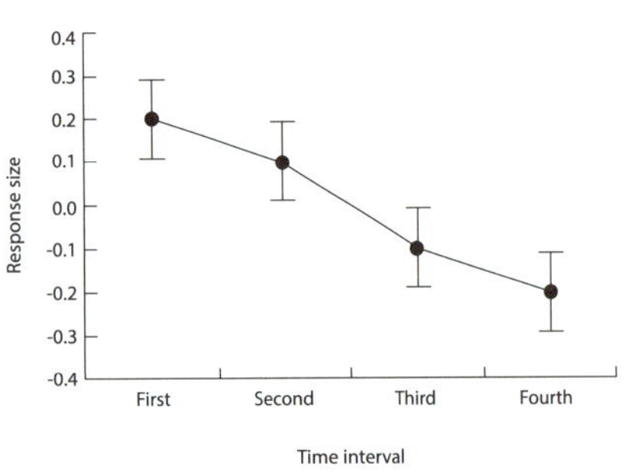

Figure 4. An example line graph with error bars. The line is generally created by interpolating the data points. Error bars represent standard errors.

F.

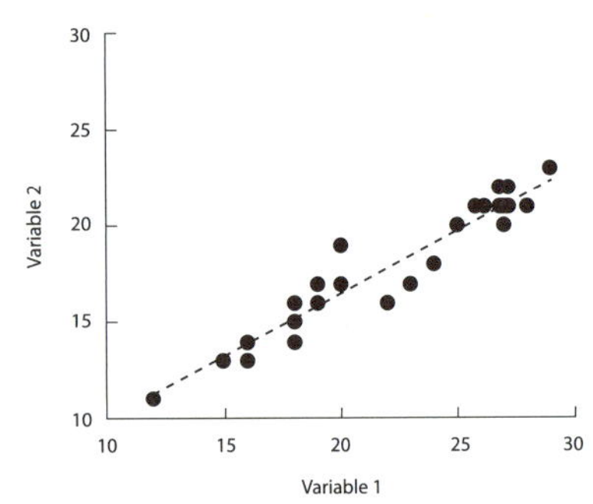

Figure 5. An example scatter plot with a linear regression line. A linear regression line is generally created by using the least square method.

8.4.1 Types of Illustrations

1 Tables

Tables are usually the best choice for reporting complex data consisting of discrete and specific values as in the example of 8.4.A.A. On the other hand, tables should not be chosen when showing a trend or pattern in the relationship between variables. By convention, the independent variables are generally listed in the columns and the dependent variables in the rows. When listing variables, they should be logically arranged. For example, when reporting the scores of two tests, the mean scores and the standard deviation of the pre-test should be placed before those of the post-test. Every table must have a deliberately written caption, which must contain the table title and any necessary information about the table, such as the following: the columns, the rows, or each entry using superscript letters, and probability information obtained from statistical analyses, and must be placed just above the table.

2 Figures

2.1 Bar Graphs

Bar graphs are used to compare the absolute values of the independent variables, and each bar can be arranged either horizontally or vertically as in the example in 8.4.A.C. The independent variables are generally placed on the horizontal axis if the bars are vertically oriented.

2.2 Line Graphs

Line graphs are used to present the relationship between quantitative variables as in the example of 8.4.A.E. By convention, the independent variable is plotted on the horizontal axis (x-axis) and the dependent variable on the vertical axis (y-axis). Line graphs are often used to show trends or patterns of Y over X.

2.3 Scatter Plots

Scatter plots are used to present how closely two quantitative variables are associated as in the example of 8.4.A.F. Each dot represents the specific value of X. There are no lines connecting the individual dots. However, a linear regression line which best fits all the dots in the scatter plot can be projected and included.

2.4 Pie Charts

Pie charts are used to present the relative size of the categorical variables to the whole in 8.4.A.D. As opposed to bar graphs, pie charts do not compare the absolute values of variables; rather, they compare the proportional values. However, the absolute values can also be included in each slice in addition to the proportional values.

2.5 Box Plots (Box and Whisker Plots)

Box plots are used to present the percentile distribution of the data; that is, they display variation in a set of data. 8.4.A.B provides an example. Box plots allow for easy comparisons of data distribution in many different groups. As seen in the right figure, box plots display five important numbers: minimum, first quartile, median, third quartile, and maximum.

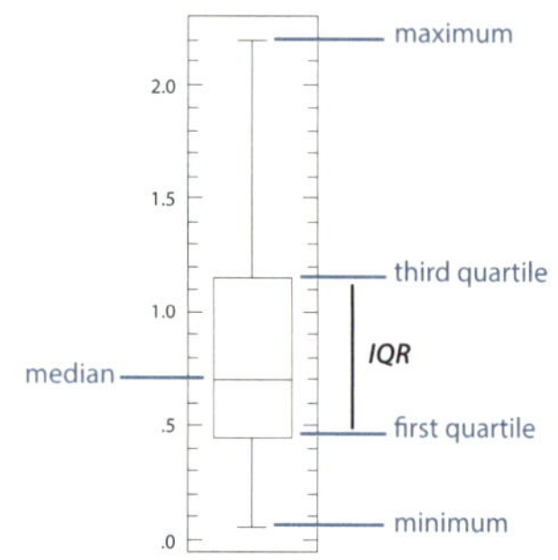

8.4.B.1

With your partner(s), read the following descriptions of each experiment and state the most appropriate form of illustration.

a. This experiment aimed to determine if there is any difference between the average GPA of freshmen and seniors.

b. This experiment aimed to examine the variation in college students' reading scores before and after priming. Pre- and post-tests were constructed to see if there was any effect of priming on college students' reading.

c. The main goal of this experiment was to see the effect of music on plant growth. The stem length changes of 30 kidney beans under different music conditions were recorded over a period of three weeks.

d. The goal of this experiment was to investigate the relationship between the commuting distance and students' GPA.

8.4.B.2

Read the sample results section from 8.3.B.2, then answer the following questions with your partner(s):

1. How many visual materials are used in the section? What are they? Is the choice of the visual materials appropriate?
2. Are the illustrations transparent and self-explanatory?
3. Are all the illustrations discussed in the text?
4. Are all the illustrations well-formatted?
5. Does the caption of each illustration include all the necessary information?

8.5 Statistical Analysis

Statistical analysis includes a broad range of concepts. The following areas represent key ideas from statistics that apply to the results section. You can find detailed information about the basic concepts of statistical terms in 5.5. You can return to 5.5 if you need further assistance.

1 Descriptive Statistics

Descriptive statistics are summative statistics that describe the basic characteristics of the data collected in a study. Through a selection of statistical numbers, descriptive statistics allow the audience to understand and compare the overall shape and the distribution of group data.

1.1 Measures of Central Tendency

1.1.1 Mean

The mean of a data set is calculated by summing up all the values in the data set and then dividing it by the number of the values. Outliers or skewed data may greatly affect the mean.

1.1.2 Median

The median of a data set is the middle value of the data set when the values are arranged in order of magnitude. The median is less affected by outliers or skewed data than the mean.

1.1.3 Mode

The mode of a data set is the most frequent value in the data set. On a bar chart, the mode corresponds to the highest value(s). The mode is the most sparsely used measure of central tendency due to the possibility of a single data set possessing multiple modes.

1.2 Measures of Dispersion

1.2.1 Variance

The variance of a data set measures the degree of the data dispersion. The variance tells the audience how far away the data in the set is from the mean.

1.2.2 Standard Deviation

The standard deviation is the most commonly used measure of dispersion. The standard deviation is defined as the square root of the variance.

1.2.3 Range

The range is the difference between the largest value and the smallest value in the data. The range is very sensitive to outliers.

1.2.4 Interquartile Range

The interquartile range is the difference between the 25th and 75th value in the data set. The interquartile range describes the distribution of the central 50% of the data. The interquartile range is relatively insensitive to outliers (see 2.5, p. 170).

2 Inferential Statistics

Inferential statistics are strong tools to test experimental hypotheses. They are stronger tools than descriptive statistics in that they allow for further generalizations about a larger population at a high level of accuracy. In order to make any statistical decisions, levels of significance must be set before conducting any statistical tests. The most frequently and widely used levels of significance are 0.05 and 0.01. If the 0.05 cutoff is used, the results are considered significant at the 0.05 level. If the 0.01 cutoff is used, the results are considered significant at the 0.01 level. The level of significance will be compared with the p-value in your statistical tests. The significance level has a direct relationship with the confidence interval of the data set, which is explained in more detail beginning on page 106 of this textbook.

To evaluate a hypothesis, use the following five steps:

a. Calculate descriptive statistics.
b. Choose an inferential test and calculate its corresponding statistic.
c. Find its associated probability (p-value) in the test result.
d. Based on the level of significance and the obtained p-value, accept or reject the null hypothesis (H_0).
e. Draw a conclusion.

2.1 T-tests

2.1.1 Independent sample T-test

The independent samples t-test compares the mean values of two data sets from two populations. By evaluating whether the mean value of one data set is the same as or different from that of the other data set, this test attempts to determine if the two data sets are from the same population or from two different populations. A t-value will be obtained in the t-test output table when conducting the statistical analysis.

2.1.2 Paired sample T-test

The paired sample t-test compares the mean values of two data sets which are matched in some way, such as two different observations taken on one population at two different points in time. For example, the paired t-test can be used to evaluate if there is any meaningful difference between pre- and post-test scores, or if there is a meaningful relationship between parents' and children's scores. A t-value will be obtained in the t-test output table when conducting the statistical analysis.

2.2 One-way ANOVA test

The one-way ANOVA test compares the mean values of three or more data sets. By evaluating whether the mean value(s) of one or more data sets is/are the same as or different from the others', this test attempts to investigate whether the data sets in the test are from one or multiple populations. For example, the one-way ANOVA test can be used to evaluate if there is any meaningful difference between the mean scores of three different classes in a school. An f-value will be obtained in the ANOVA-test output table. Additional post-hoc tests must be conducted in order to see which particular pair(s) of data sets have meaningfully different mean values.

2.3 Pearson's Correlation (r)

Pearson's correlation (r) is used to describe how closely and tightly the quantitative values of two variables are associated. The value of Pearson's correlation coefficient r can range from -1 and 1. As seen in the following figures, if $|r| = 1$, both variables have a perfect relationship; if $r = 0$, the two variables have no relationship at all. The +/- symbols indicate the directionality of the relationship between variables as seen in the following figures. In other words, if r is a negative value, the two variables have a negative correlation, and vice versa.

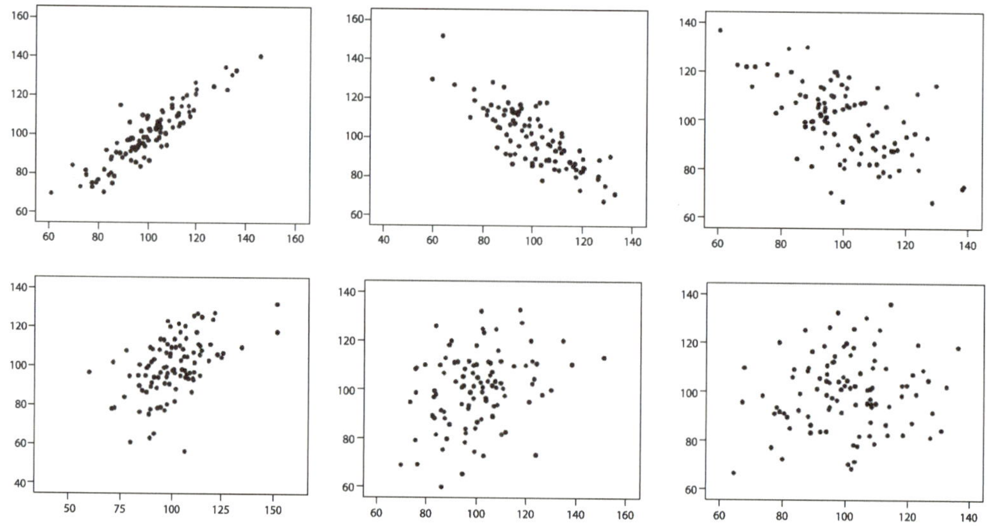

8.5.A

Examine the scatter plots above and answer the following questions.

1. Find the scatter plots which demonstrate a positive correlation between variables.
2. Find the scatter plots which demonstrate a negative correlation between variables.
3. Which scatter plot has the strongest correlation between variables?
4. Which scatter plot has the weakest correlation between variables?

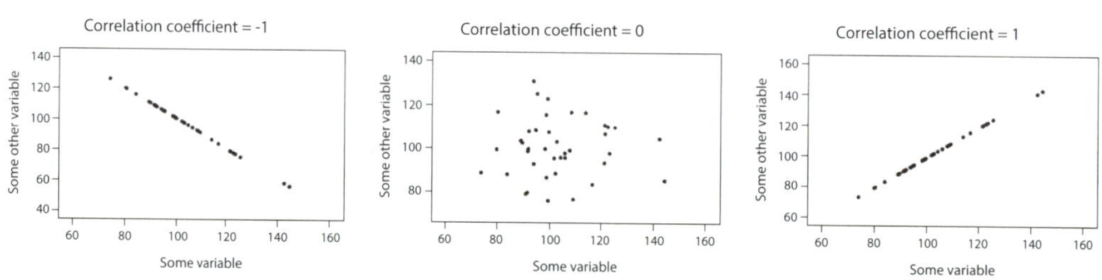

8.6 Reading

The following has been extracted and adapted from: Peters, J.C., Polsky, S., Stark, R., Zhaoxing, P., & Hill, J.O. (2014). *Appetite*, *79*, 183-188.

8.6.A

Read the research paper excerpt and reflect on answers to questions 1-4 that follow.

The Influence of Herbs and Spices on Overall Liking of Reduced Fat Food

Results

[1] Among 154 individuals consented to the study, five did not go on to participate in the study and one was excluded due to pregnancy, leaving 148 for our final analyses (96.1%). [2] There were no significant differences in demographic characteristics or FFQ dietary habits between individuals who participated in the study and those who did not (data not shown). [3] Baseline characteristics and dietary habits of participants are shown in Table 2. [4] The mean body mass index (BMI), calculated from self-reported weight and height on the 2005 Block FFQ, was 24.4 kg/m^2, with a minimum value of 17.5 and a maximum value of 41.6 kg/m^2 for the total cohort. [5] Based on the Block FFQ, the percentages of calories consumed as fat and as saturated fat were 36% and 11%, respectively, which are consistent with national data sets that report consumption of 33–38% of total calories from

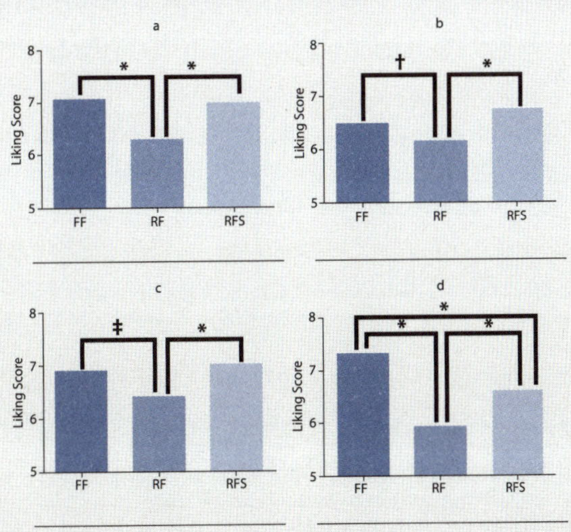

Figure 1. Liking scores by test meal condition. Liking scores for full fat (FF), reduced fat with no added spice (RF), and reduced fat plus spice (RFS) meal conditions are presented. *P ≤ 0.0002; †P = 0.02; ‡P = 0.002.

fat and 11–13% of total calories from saturated fat in US adults (The National Health and Nutrition Examination Survey [NHANES]) (Austin, Ogden, & Hill, 2011; Kris-Etherton et al., 2012; Wright & Wang, 2010). [6] These results indicate that the dietary habits of the subject population enrolled are not dissimilar from those of the American population as a whole.

[7] Among the 148 participants, 140 attended sessions for all three test meal conditions, but four participants missed the FF session, two missed the RF session, and two missed the RFS session. [8] Absolute liking scores for the full fat meal were typical of food tasting studies, with the mean being 7.05 units on a 9-point Likert scale, establishing that the full fat meal without additional spices was well liked overall. [9] For the overall meal, reducing fat caused a significant drop in overall liking (6.29 RF vs. 7.05 FF, P < 0.0001, **see Fig. _____**). [10] Adding herbs and spices to the reduced fat meal completely attenuated the decline in meal liking scores such that the RFS condition was not significantly different from the FF condition (6.98 RFS vs. 7.05 FF, P = 0.6026). Similar findings were obtained for the meatloaf and vegetable items when looked at separately (**see Fig. _____**). [11] Mean Likert scores for the overall meal and individual test meal items are shown in Table 3. [12] Numerically, liking scores for the RFS meatloaf and vegetables trended higher than for the FF versions, although they were not significantly different. [13] Liking scores for both FF and RFS meatloaf and vegetables were significantly greater than for RF.

[14] The addition of herbs and spices to the creamy pasta did not completely restore liking to the level obtained for the FF condition (6.61 RFS vs. 7.33 FF, P < 0.0001, **see _____**). [15] All three pasta treatments were significantly different from each other with FF scoring the highest, RF the lowest, and RFS in between (5.94 RF vs. 7.33 FF, P < 0.0001; 5.94 RF vs. 6.61 RFS, P < 0.0001).

[16] There were no significant differences in the amount of the meal consumed across the three test conditions as seen in Table 3. [17] Mean consumption was approximately 85% of the food provided. This suggests that all the meal conditions were generally liked.

Table 3
Mean Likert scores for test meal items and percentage of meal eaten by test meal condition.

Test meal item	Mean score		
	Full fat	Reduced fat	Reduced fat with spice
Overall meal	7.05[a]	6.29[b]	6.98
Meatloaf	6.51[c]	6.15[b]	6.76
Vegetable side dish	6.91[d]	6.42[e]	7.02
Pasta side dish	7.33[a]	5.94[b]	6.61[f]
Mean percentage of meal eaten	85.9	83.7	84.9

[a] $P < 0.0001$ for difference from reduced fat.
[b] $P \leq 0.0001$ for difference from reduced fat with spice.
[c] $P < 0.02$ for difference from reduced fat.
[d] $P = 0.002$ for difference from reduced fat.
[e] $P = 0.0002$ for difference from reduced fat with spice.
[f] $P < 0.0001$ for difference from full fat.

With your partner(s), do the following exercise:

1. Results Model: What role does each sentence in the results section play? Go back to the results model in 8.3 and match each sentence in the sample with the descriptions of the model.

Sentence 1 ____

Sentence 2 ____

Sentence 3 ____

Sentence 4 ____

Sentence 5 ____

Sentence 6 ____

Sentence 7 ____

Sentence 8 ____

Sentence 9 ____

Sentence 10 ____

Sentence 11 ____

Sentence 12 ____

Sentence 13 ____

Sentence 14 ____

Sentence 15 ____

Sentence 16 ____

Sentence 17 ____

2. What is the primary verb tense used in the sample? What other tense(s) is(are) used and where? Discuss why different tenses are used in the results section.

3. The figure in 8.6.A does not include labels for the horizontal axes, and there are three underlined gaps in the body of the text. Read the excerpt again and locate where the corresponding information for the labels is discussed. Then complete the horizontal axes in the figure with that information and fill in the three underlined gaps within the body of the text.

4. In this sample results section, there is no explicit interpretation of the results. If you were the author of this paper, how would you interpret the results? Write one or two sentences explaining the meaning of the results.

____

____

____

8.7 Writing

8.7.A

The following 'Summary of methodology' and tables were taken from a paper entitled "The Effect of Music and Lyrics on Reading Comprehension and Math Tests" and modified for this textbook. Look at the result tables carefully and try to write a sample result section on your own.

Summary of methodology

Number of participants: 20 college students

Data collection method:

20 college students came to a computer lab and wore a headset. Then half of the students took a math test while listening to music without lyrics. After a 30 minute break, they took another math test while listening to music with lyrics. The other half took the same math test while listening to music with lyrics first and then music without lyrics. The same 20 students came to the same computer lab one week after the math tests. This time they took the reading comprehension test following the same procedure as the math test.

Table 1. The mean scores (total score = 10) and standard deviations of participants' reading comprehension test and math test while listening to music with and without lyrics.

Music with lyrics		Music without lyrics	
Average Reading Score (S.D.)	Average Math Score (S.D.)	Average Reading Score (S.D.)	Average Math Score (S.D.)
4.867 (0.640)	7.667 (0.976)	5.056 (0.639)	7.056 (1.162)

Table 2. The results of the paired t-test between reading and math scores with and without music.

	Reading		Math	
	t	p	t	p
Music without lyrics – Music with lyrics	2.051	0.056	-6.298	< 0.001

Opening of the results section

Body of the results section

Closure of the results section

Read the following sample of a results section explaining the outcome of the bubble wrap study.

The Insulation Performance of Bubble Wrap Attached to Windows

Results

The insulation efficiency of bubble wrap was estimated by measuring the temperature differences (ΔT) between the inside and outside of the Styrofoam cubic box; this determined the optimal number of bubble wrap layers. Fig. 1 indicates that temperature differences between the inside and the outside of the cubic box increased as the number of bubble wrap layers increased. The largest temperature difference (14.7 °C) was recorded when the cubic box was covered with five layers of the bubble wrap, while the smallest (12.3 °C) was measured when there was no bubble wrap.

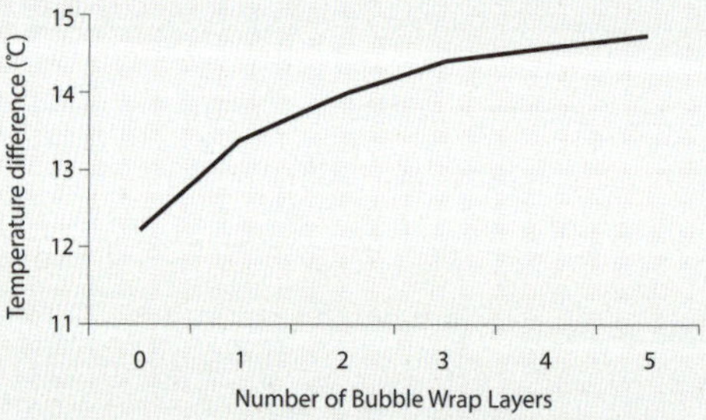

Figure 1. Temperature differences between the inside and the outside of the Styrofoam cubic box (ΔT, °C) depending on the number of bubble wrap layers.

The slopes of temperature differences ($\Delta T_n - \Delta T_{n-1}$) were then calculated in order to estimate the optimal number of bubble wrap layers as reported in Table 1. As can be seen, the slope change of the temperature differences between the inside and the outside of the cubic box was the largest (1.13 °C) when the cubic box was wrapped with one layer of the bubble wrap; however, it was the smallest (0.14 °C) when the bubble wrap layers increased from four to five. Although a series of t-tests did not show any significant differences in temperature changes ($t = 1.853$, $p = 0.12$), the slopes of the temperature difference changed substantially as the number of bubble wrap layers increased to three. As the layers increased to four and then five, however, the slope changes gradually decreased.

Table 1. The slopes of the temperature difference depending on the number of bubble wrap layers.

Layer Increment	0 → 1	1 → 2	2 → 3	3 → 4	4 → 5
$\Delta T_n - \Delta T_{n-1}$ (℃)	1.13	0.60	0.43	0.19	0.14

8.7.B

Search for a video clip by inputting the keywords "simple paper chromatography," watch the video, and write the results section of the experiment.

Re-read the results section of the bubble wrap experiment described above. Then, using a similar structure, write the results of the paper chromatography experiment.

The opening of the results section

The body of the results section

The closure of the results section

Writing Your Results Section

- This is the end of Chapter 8. It is now time for you to think about the results section that you will write for your research paper.
- Before you start drafting, you should go through the pre-writing process and create a clear outline that shows the coherence (logical connection) of each part of the stages in the process you are writing about.
- You should write this section of your research paper in three sections, although this does not necessarily mean that it will comprise three paragraphs.
- After you have created your rough draft, use the revision checklist below to make editorial changes.

Revision Checklist

Did you ...

☐ report the results of the research logically and thoroughly without excessive interpretation?

☐ write in the past tense when describing the results?

☐ use the active and passive voice where appropriate?

☐ use parallel structures where appropriate?

☐ analyze the data with appropriate statistical analyses?

☐ report the results with appropriate illustrations?

☐ answer the hypotheses established in the research design?

9 Discussion/Conclusion

Analyzing, interpreting, and assessing the design and results of your research project

Learning Outcomes:

- to understand the purpose of a discussion/conclusion section
- to learn the goals of the discussion/conclusion section
- to learn and use modals in order to interpret and assess your results
- to learn and use inference verbs to interpret and assess your results
- to learn how to structure your discussion/conclusion section
- to learn how to read and understand a discussion/conclusion section
- to write a thorough and insightful discussion/conclusion section

9.1 Overview

Now that you have compiled and reported the results of your research project, you now need to focus on the task of interpreting and explaining the outcome.

The discussion/conclusion section has a number of important aims that we will examine in this chapter, but it could easily be summarized by the following questions:

(1) What is the deeper meaning of the results of your research?

(2) What did you learn from your research project?

(3) What kind of knowledge or insight does your research project contribute to your field?

Before we proceed any further, it should be noted that many scientific research papers divide the discussion and conclusion sections into two distinct areas. In this textbook, however, the two sections are combined.

A discussion/conclusion section should seek to achieve the following goals:

- It should revisit previous sections in the paper.
- It should expand upon the results section by making inferences about the data and examining the wider implications of your research.
- It should make a clear conclusion about the original hypothesis.
- It should state the achievement of your research project and how it contributed to the knowledge and future of your field.
- It should examine the strengths, weakness, and limitations of your research project.

To clarify each of these specific points, the discussion/conclusion section should first act as a summary and reflection of the entire research project. Key ideas from the introduction, methodology, and results sections should therefore be revisited to both refresh the reader's memory and to emphasize crucial concepts which relate to the purpose of your research. Next, the discussion/conclusion section should seek to examine the deeper meaning of the data in your research. Recall from the results section that the field of statistics can be broadly classified into two areas: descriptive and inferential. In general, while the results section does include some kind of inferential analysis, it typically places a greater emphasis on the descriptive side of statistics. In other words, it focuses on the area of statistics that seeks to describe data, but not to make additional assumptions about what it means or suggests about the wider population from which it originates. The discussion/conclusion section, on the other hand, should place a stronger emphasis on inferential statistics.

As explained in the results chapter, an important aspect of inferential statistics is that it allows us to make a clear conclusion about our original hypothesis. Naturally, the discussion/conclusion section should make a final conclusion about whether the original predictions you made in your research were proven correct, and should also examine why the data either conformed to or conflicted with your original prediction. This should lead to a broader analysis of the contribution your research has made to your field, as well as a comparison of your research project's achievements with those of previous research projects.

Lastly, the discussion/conclusion section should include some level of self-assessment. Some aspects of your research project may have worked very well, but others may have proven to be problematic and should be revised, adjusted, or perhaps even eliminated in the future. In addition to the strengths and weaknesses of your research, you should also examine its limitations. The scope of your research might allow you to make definitive statements about some groups of people, objects, or concepts, but not all of them. The scope should therefore be directly mentioned in this section, with possible suggestions for improving it in the future.

9.2 Purpose

9.2.A

Consider the following sample discussion/conclusion section and answer the questions that follow.

The Insulation Performance of Bubble Wrap Attached to Windows

Discussion/Conclusion

Prior research has documented the effect of qualitative factors of bubble wrap such as air tightness (Bae et al., 2017) and type (Seo, 2015) in improving insulation efficiency. However, these studies have either been purely theoretical or have focused on specialized bubble wrap which is not available to normal consumers. This study was done to investigate questions about multilayered bubble wrap and give practical advice to consumers; hence, it has a different focus from the aforementioned studies. Previous experiments have indicated that the insulation performance improved as the number of layers increased, but the improvement progressively decreased with the number of layers. Ultimately, statistical inference tests demonstrated that there was a significant improvement up to the third layer, but not beyond it. The negligible improvement that was found in four or more layers must be due to the economic principle of diminishing returns.

However, the results of this study do not necessarily suggest that everyone should attach three layers of bubble wrap to their window. One layer of insulation might be sufficient in some cases (such as one's economic circumstances) and, if so, it is not recommended to add more. Adding a second or third layer of insulated bubble wrap still saves energy efficiently, but beyond that the economic efficiency declines. Two sheets of bubble wrap cost twice as much as one, but the insulation efficiency improves at a much smaller rate.

This study had a number of strengths. The first major advantage was that due to the simplicity in the test's design, analyzing the results was a very straightforward process which almost entirely involved examining the temperature difference, or ΔT. The result ΔT is easily understood and interpreted; furthermore, it has a clear relationship with basic scientific theories from thermodynamics and other fields. Another notable benefit is that the results obtained from the study can be easily applied in real life. However, some limitations are worth noting. The most significant drawback was that this study did not consider light transmittance in relation to insulation performance. Both thermal conductivity and light transmittance should be considered when measuring the insulation performance of a window attached insulation sheet as Zhang et al. (2016) proposed. The ideal insulator is one with low thermal conductivity and high light transmittance. However, only the thermal conductivity was tested in this study due to a lack of equipment. In adding an extra layer, the conductivity increases and transmittance decreases; thus, it has an inverse effect. For this reason, the results from the current experiment may have overestimated the insulation performance. Future studies which include light transmittance are needed to ensure greater accuracy. The next issue is that this study only used one type of bubble wrap. Different results may occur with different kinds of bubble wrap. For this experiment, the formula would have to be newly constructed in a different form since the thickness L of each bubble wrap varies, and ΔT could not be used. Future studies should therefore include a more diverse range of bubble wrap types.

9.2.B Discussion and Analysis

1. Where do we see references to other sections in the research paper?
2. Where do we see an analysis of the deeper meaning of the data; i.e. a usage of inferential statistics?
3. What is the author's conclusion about the research project?
4. What specific comparisons does the author make to previous research? What is the purpose of the comparison?
5. What are the strengths, weaknesses, and limitations of the research project?
6. What is the function of the word 'must' in the last sentence of the first paragraph?
7. In the third paragraph, the author writes, "For this reason, the results from the current experiment may have overestimated the insulation performance." What is the function of the word 'may' in this sentence?
8. What is the function of the word 'should' in the concluding sentence?

9.3 Language

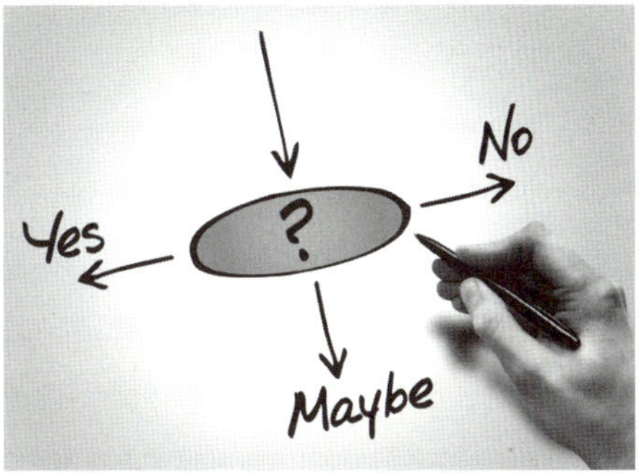

In the sample discussion/conclusion discussion and analysis from 9.2.B, you considered the function of a number of words such as 'must', 'may', and 'should'. These words all fall into a broad grammatical category called *modal verbs*. Modal verbs can serve a range of functions in English, but the two main uses that are most relevant to scientific writing are to express *degree of certainty* and *necessity*.

As we have previously noted, one of the primary aims of the discussion/conclusion section is to make conclusions about the results of our research. In other words, we are making some kind of *truth claim*; recall from Chapter 5 our discussion on what constitutes truth in science. Our degree of certainty in the truth statements we make will range from weak to strong, depending on the claim, and modals serve as an ideal language form to express our degree of certainty.

Let us first turn our attention to modals which are used to make a relatively weak truth claim.

❖ Present tense usage of 'may', 'can', and 'might'

Before proceeding with the main ideas of this section, we need to qualify our usage of the words 'may', 'can', and 'might'. These words are often used to request permission (as in "May I ask you a question?" or "Can you help me with my scientific research paper?"), but that function is not applicable to scientific writing. Instead, we are strictly concerned with the second usage: the expression of possibility or potential when making an educated guess.

9.3.A

Consider the following statements as examples:

1. In any clinical trial, a change in a patient's condition *may be* due to the placebo effect.

2. Violent video games *can lead* to increased aggression.
3. The increase in pollution *might result from* the use of plastic at the factory.

The modal verbs in the above sentences serve as *auxiliary verbs* which modify the meaning of the main verb in the sentence; for example, consider how the meaning of #2 changes if we delete the word 'can'. In each of the three cases above, we can see that the author is *hedging* the main idea. To 'hedge' means to confine or restrict a condition, or set of conditions, for the purpose of minimizing risk. In this case, the risk involves making a truth claim that is, in fact, wrong. Hence, the three modal verbs above are used when we are only somewhat certain of the truth claim we are making.

There are, in fact, small differences between the modals. 'Might' is considered a bit weaker than 'may' in tone. Moreover, 'can' includes the idea of having the ability to do something.

❖ Negative forms of the present tense usage of 'may', 'can', and 'might'

Next, we will consider how to form the negative present tense form of these modal verbs, as in the following two examples:

4. In any clinical trial, a change in a test subject's condition *may not be due* to the drug itself.
5. The increase in pollution *might not result from* the use of plastic at the factory.

Notice how Sentences 1 and 4 both express similar ideas, but in different ways. We can make a similar observation about Sentences 3 and 5.

In each case, we can substitute the words 'is possibly' for the modal verbs. Hence, 'may not' and 'might not' both have precisely the same meaning: 'is possibly not'.

However, we have not yet considered the negative form of the modal verb 'can'. This is because 'cannot' has a completely different meaning from 'may not' or 'might not'. (Note: we always write 'cannot' as one word, unlike the negative forms of 'may' and 'might').

Consider the negative form of Sentence 2 above:

6. The results indicate that violent video games *cannot lead* to increased aggression.

How does the meaning of 'cannot' differ from 'may not' or 'might not'? You can try substituting either of the latter two options into the above sentence as a comparison point.

We can see here that 'is possibly not' cannot be used as a substitute for 'cannot'. Instead, we have to use a substitute such as 'is definitely not'. 'Cannot', therefore, is used to express the idea of impossibility. Such a claim is in fact a strong claim, and therefore not a hedge at all; hence, 'cannot' represents an exception to our general rule that 'may', 'can', and 'might' are used to hedge our truth claims.

❖ Past tense usage of 'may', 'can', and 'might'

To create the past form of 'may' or 'might', we add the word 'have', as in the following examples:

7. For this clinical trial, the change in our test subjects' condition *may have been due* to the placebo effect.
8. The results indicate that violent video games *could have led* to increased aggression.
9. The increase in pollution *might have resulted from* the use of plastic at the factory.

Note the relationship between Sentences 1 and 7, 2 and 8, and 3 and 9. The present tense usage expresses the idea in its general or universal form, while the past tense usage expresses the idea as it occurred during a single event in the past.

Moreover, notice that we use 'could' – the past tense form of 'can' – to form the past tense for this modal verb.

Finally, notice that the main verb of the sentence – 'be', 'lead', and 'result', in this case – needs to be changed to its past participle form.

❖ Negative forms of the past tense usage of 'may', 'can', and 'might'

Finally, we will consider how to form the negative past tense form of these modal verbs. It follows a combination of the previous rules we have considered:

10. For this clinical trial, the change in our test subjects' condition *may not have been due* to the drug itself.
11. The results indicate that violent video games *could not have led* to increased aggression.

12. The increase in pollution *might not have resulted from* the use of plastic at the factory.

How do the three truth claims above combine previously discussed rules for the modal verbs 'may', 'can', and 'might'?

❖ Present tense usage of 'must'

The modal verb 'must' is used to deliver a much stronger truth claim than 'may', 'can', and 'might'. Like the previous section, we do need to qualify our usage of this verb; we are not including instances of 'must' such as the following: "Scientific research papers must include data analysis." In these cases, the writer is both expressing a necessary condition and delivering an order to the reader. Typically, writers use the modal 'should' – which is a bit softer in tone and is interpreted more as advice than an order – in place of 'must' in these instances. The modal 'should' will be explained in more detail in a later section.

'Must' is also used to express the fact that we are almost completely certain of the truth claim we are making. The fact that we are using the modal 'must' means that our statement is still considered an inference and not an objective fact, but we nevertheless have a very high level of confidence in our claim. For example, consider the following statements:

1. In these cases, the change in the patient's condition *must be due* to the placebo effect.
2. According to our research, violent video games *must lead* to increased aggression.
3. The increase in pollution *must result from* the use of plastic at the factory.

In each case, the writer is making a strong truth claim, which is most likely based on strong statistical evidence.

❖ Negative forms of the present tense usage of 'must'

Next, we will consider how to form the negative present tense form of 'must', as in the following examples:

4. In these cases, the change in the patient's condition *must not be due* to the placebo effect.

5. According to our research, violent video games *must not lead* to increased aggression.
6. The increase in pollution *must not result from* the use of plastic at the factory.

We might say that the writer is approximately 90-95% confident in these negative truth claims. Remember that if we are 100% certain, 'cannot' should be used instead of 'must not'.

❖ Past tense usage of "must'

To create the past tense, we follow the same rules for 'must' that we do for 'may', 'can', and 'might', as in the following examples:

7. For this clinical trial, the change in our test subjects' condition *must have been due* to the placebo effect.
8. The results indicate that violent video games *must have led* to increased aggression.
9. The increase in pollution *must have resulted from* the use of plastic at the factory.

As you did previously, note the relationship between Sentences 1 and 7, 2 and 8, and 3 and 9. What is the specific difference between each of the sentence pairs?

❖ Negative forms of the past tense usage of 'must'

Finally, we form the negative past tense form of 'must' in the same manner that we did with 'may', 'can', and 'might'.

10. For this clinical trial, the change in our test subjects' condition *must not have been due* to the drug itself.
11. The results indicate that violent video games *must not have led* to increased aggression.
12. The increase in pollution *must not have resulted from* the use of plastic at the factory.

❖ Present tense usage of 'should'

The final modal verb that we will consider is 'should'. Unlike the previous modal verbs, we are going to consider two distinct functions of 'should' in this section. Consider the following two uses in the present tense.

1. As long as the material is kept below 30 ℃, it *should remain* stable.
2. The glass beakers *should be thoroughly cleaned* before conducting the experiment.

What is the specific function of 'should' in each sentence above?

In the first sentence, 'should' expresses an expectation or a prediction. In this case, the writer is stating that it is extremely likely that the device will remain stable if the material is kept below 30 ℃. It is possible that an exception could occur (such as an explosion), but that would be extremely surprising.

The second sentence, on the other hand, represents a form of advice. The writer is essentially stating, "I advise you to thoroughly cleanse the glass beakers before conducting the experiment."

❖ Negative forms of the present tense usage of 'should'

The negative present tense for of "should" follows the same rules that we previously covered.

3. As long as the material is kept below 30 degrees Celsius, it *should not* explode.
4. The glass beakers *should not have* any dust or residue on them before conducting the experiment.

❖ Past tense usage of 'should'

To create the past tense, we follow the same rules for 'should' that we do for all other modal verbs, as in the following examples.

5. Given the fact that the material was kept below 30 degrees Celsius, it *should have remained* stable.
6. The glass beakers *should have been thoroughly cleaned* before conducting the experiment.

Each of the sentences above seem to have an implied idea that is not directly stated. What is the underlying idea of each sentence above?

In Sentence 5, the writer is expressing an expectation about the past. This might seem counterintuitive; how can we express an expectation about something that has already

happened? In most cases, we are expressing a conflict between what we *expected* to happen in the past and what *actually* happened in the past. Hence, it appears that the material in Sentence 5 did not, in fact, remain stable when the experiment was performed. The writer is surprised at this occurrence, and is using the past form of 'should' to express this.

In Sentence 6, the writer is expressing a judgment about what happened. It is clear from the language that the glass beakers were not thoroughly cleaned before the experiment was conducted, which was contrary to the rules of the laboratory.

❖ Negative forms of the past tense usage of 'should'

To create the negative past tense, we follow the same rules for 'should' that we do for all other modal verbs, as in the following examples.

7. Given the fact that the material was kept below 30 degrees Celsius, it *should not have exploded.*
8. The glass beakers *should not have had* any dirt or residue on them before conducting the experiment.

Why is the negative past tense form of 'should' being used in each sentence above? What actually happened in each case?

9.3.B Practice

Rewrite each sentence with an appropriate modal verb. Think carefully about the right verb tense and whether or not the negative form should be used in each case.

1. Perhaps the increase in the test subjects' reading scores was due to their exposure to classical music.

   ______________________________.

2. We felt sure that the increase in the test subjects' reading scores was due to their exposure to classical music.

   ______________________________.

3. There is no way that the increase in the test subjects' reading scores was due to their exposure to classical music.

   ______________________________.

4. We do not expect the test subjects' reading scores to increase as a result of their exposure to classical music.

   ______________________________.

5. It is possible that the increase in the test subjects' reading scores was not a consequence of their exposure to classical music.

   ______________________________.

6. I advise your research team to select test subjects from a more diverse age range in the future.

   ______________________________.

7. I think it was a poor idea to select your test subjects from such a narrow age range.

   ______________________________.

9.4 Goals and Structure

In the beginning of this chapter, we discussed the main aims of the discussion/conclusion section. To review this information, your discussion/conclusion section should seek to achieve the following:

a. Overview prior and relevant research
b. Review key points from the introduction and methodology sections
c. Review key results from the research study
d. Interpret the results by examining their underlying meaning via inferential statistics
e. Compare the current study to previous research
f. Explain the achievement or contribution of the research study to the field
g. Explain possible applications of the research study
h. Explain the strengths of the research study
i. Explain the specific weaknesses and limitations of the research study
j. Suggest possible improvements of the research study for the future

In general, the points listed above should be followed in sequence; doing so will create a clear and easy-to-follow structure in your discussion/conclusion section.

While the number of paragraphs you write in this section is ultimately your choice, you might consider organizing this section in the same three-part structure mentioned in the methodology section (see 7.4).

❖ Opening of the discussion/conclusion section

The opening of the discussion/conclusion section should mostly focus on a review of the research study. Hence, this section could include the following:

- an overview of prior research that has been done in your field
- a review of key points from both the introduction and methodology sections
- a review of key results from your research study

❖ Body of the discussion/conclusion section

The body of the discussion/conclusion section should mostly focus on the interpretation of the results of your study, as well as an examination of how your study contributes to the knowledge in your field. Hence, this section could include the following:

- an interpretation of the results of your study through the use of inferential statistics
- a comparison of your study to previous research
- an explanation of the specific achievement or contribution your study has made to your field
- an explanation of possible applications of your research study

❖ Closure of the discussion/conclusion section

The closure of your discussion/conclusion section should focus on self-assessment. Hence, this section could include the following:

- an explanation of the strengths of your study
- an explanation of the weaknesses and limitations of your study
- suggestions for possible improvements of your study in the future

9.5 Reading

The following has been extracted and adapted from: Peters, J.C., Polsky, S., Stark, R., Zhaoxing, P., & Hill, J.O. (2014). *Appetite*, *79*, 183-188.

9.5.A

Read the following discussion/conclusion and examine how each sentence pertains to a part of the discussion/conclusion section structure introduced in 9.4.

The Influence of Herbs and Spices on Overall Liking of Reduced Fat Food

Discussion/Conclusion

[1] In this study, the addition of herbs and spices to reduced fat foods restored the liking of the overall meal to that of the full fat version of the meal, which was consistent with the hypothesis. [2] On an individual meal item basis this was also true for the meatloaf entrée and vegetable side dish, with a trend for a higher liking of foods that included the herbs and spices. [3] The reduced fat pasta side dish with herbs and spices was rated higher than the reduced fat dish without herbs and spices, but still not equally to the full fat version.

[4] Several factors have been associated with the liking of meat products. [5] One previous study assessed the palatability characteristics of overall liking, tenderness, juiciness, and flavor liking among consumers tasting beef strip loin steaks of varying fat content. (O'Quinn, Brooks, Polkinghorne, Garmyn, Johnson, Starkey, Rathmann, & Miller, 2012). [6] All scores increased with increasing beef fat content. [7] Furthermore, among the characteristics tested, overall liking was most highly correlated with flavor liking. [8] Spices increase food flavor, which may be one explanation for the equal liking for FF and RFS meatloaf entrée items in our study. [9] As for vegetable liking, another study identified barriers and facilitators to adherence to the 2010 Dietary Guidelines for Americans. (Nicklas, Jahns, Bogle, Chester, Giovanni, Klurfeld, Laugero, Liu, Lopez, & Tucker, 2013). [10] Adult subjects ranked taste and bad taste as big barriers to meeting guidelines for vegetable consumption (6.2 and 5.7, respectively where a score of 10 indicates the biggest barrier). [11] Moreover, they ranked "liking the vegetables" as the second highest ranked facilitator to meeting those guidelines (9.8 out of 10). [12] In our study, fat variation for the vegetable dish was a result of the amount of butter being reduced in the RF and RFS test conditions, compared with the FF. [13] Consumers liked the FF and RFS vegetable side dishes significantly more than RF, but liked the FF and RFS dishes equally well. [14] These data suggest that the addition of herbs and spices to

reduced fat vegetables may be a strategy to improve adoption and adherence to national dietary guidelines.

[15] This study has several strengths. [16] Like most Americans, our study participants habitually consume diets higher in fat than recommended by national guidelines of committees. [17] Thus, a lack of significant differences in liking ratings between FF and RFS conditions is not a reflection of consumer dietary habits being different than those of the general population. [18] Moreover, participants were required to have a significant wash-out period of at least 48 hours between tastings of test meal conditions rather than conduct side-by-side, same day comparisons that may have unblinded participants to the variation of fat content in the meals.

[19] This study did have some limitations. [20] First, although participants were not informed what the specific differences in fat, herb, and spice content was in the test meal items, some spices were visible in RFS test items. [21] It is possible that the slight variation in food presentation with spices being visible in RFS test items affected consumer liking scores. [22] Another potential issue was that we did not include a test condition with full-fat and added herbs and spices, as the addition of herbs and spices to a full-fat condition would not directly benefit an exploration of our strategy to improve palatability of reduced-fat foods. [23] Future studies could consider adding such a test condition to further examine whether the addition of herbs and spices can enhance the palatability of food containing different quantities of fat. [24] Finally, while the habitual dietary intake of our participants was similar to that of the general American population, we did not have similar representations of sexes, races, and ethnicities.

[25] In our study, the FF and RFS test meals received similar overall liking ratings and there were no differences between the amounts of food eaten. [26] This finding suggests that incorporating spices into reduced fat items could be a potential strategy for helping Americans meet the US dietary guidelines for fat and saturated fat without having to sacrifice liking. [27] Reducing total fat intake could help people manage their overall calorie intake, which could help in body weight management, a high priority for many people. [28] Herbs and spices also show promise for increasing vegetable intake. [29] Further studies are needed to extend these findings to meals with different food composition and to longer term examination of whether herbs and spices can promote healthier eating in the context of peoples' daily lives.

References

O'Quinn, T.G., Brooks, J.C., Polkinghorne, R.J., Garmyn, A.J., Johnson, B.J., Starkey, J.D., Rathmann, R.J., & Miller M.F. (2012). Consumer assessment of beef strip loin steaks of varying fat levels. *Journal of Animal Science*, *90*(2), 626–634. doi:10.2527/jas.2011-4282.

Nicklas, T.A., Jahns, L., Bogle, M.L., Chester, D.N., Giovanni, M., Klurfeld, D.M., Laugero, K., Liu, Y., Lopez, S., & Tucker, K.L. (2013). Barriers and facilitators for consumer adherence to the dietary guidelines for Americans. The HEALTH Study. *Journal of the Academy of Nutrition and Dietetics*, *113*(10), 1317–1331. doi:10.1016/j.jand.2013.05.004.

9.5.B Discussion

With your partner(s), do the following:

1. Relate individual sentences to the key goals stated in Section 9.4. For example, which sentences relate to Point A? Which sentences relate to Point B? Try to find examples of all the points covered in this section (a-j).

2. Identify the general structure of the above discussion/conclusion section. Where does the introduction end and the body begin? Where does the body end and the conclusion begin?

3. Find specific examples of modal verbs in the discussion/conclusion section above and discuss the purpose they serve.

9.6. Writing

9.6.A

Recall from Section 8.7.A your analysis of the research project entitled "The Effect of Music and Lyrics on Reading Comprehension and Math Tests." The summary of the methodology and results are included in this section again. Write a discussion/conclusion section for this research project based on the information in the tables below, as well as your previous analysis from Chapter 8. Try to include all of the information mentioned from Section 9.4.

Summary of methodology

Number of participants: 20 college students

Data collection method:
20 college students came to a computer lab and wore a headset. Then half of the students took a math test while listening to music without lyrics. After a 30 min break, they took another math test while listening to music with lyrics. The other half took the same math test while listening to music with lyrics first and then music without lyrics. The same 20 students came to the same computer lab one week after the math tests. This time they took the reading comprehension test following the same procedure as the math test.

Table 1. The mean scores (total score = 10) and the standard deviations of participants' reading comprehension test and math test while listening to music with and without lyrics.

Music with lyrics		Music without lyrics	
Average Reading Score (S.D.)	Average Math Score (S.D.)	Average Reading Score (S.D.)	Average Math Score (S.D.)
4.867 (0.640)	7.667 (0.976)	5.056 (0.639)	7.056 (1.162)

Table 2. The results of the paired t-test between reading and math scores with and without music.

	Reading		Math	
	t	p	t	p
Music without lyrics – Music with lyrics	2.051	0.056	-6.298	< 0.001

Opening of the discussion/conclusion section

Body of the discussion/conclusion section

Closure of the discussion/conclusion section

Outlining and Writing Your Discussion/Conclusion Section

- This is the end of Chapter 9. It is now time for you to think about the discussion/conclusion section that you will write for your assignment.
- You should first spend time using inferential statistics to interpret and explain your data.
- You should pay attention to modal verb usage when determining the strength of your claims.
- Before you start drafting, you should go through the pre-writing process and create a clear outline that shows the coherence (logical connection) of each part of the stages in the process you are writing about.
- After you have created your rough draft, use the revision checklist below to make editorial changes.

Revision Checklist

Did you ...

☐ make clear references to your introduction and methodology sections?

☐ use inferential statistics to examine the deeper meaning of your results?

☐ compare your research with previous research studies?

☐ state the achievement and possible applications of your research study?

☐ examine the strengths and weaknesses of your research study?

⑩ Abstract

Summarizing and reporting the key elements of your research

Learning Outcomes:

- to understand the purpose of an abstract in a scientific research paper
- to learn the goals of the abstract
- to revisit common verb tenses that are used with each section of a scientific research paper
- to learn how to structure your abstract
- to learn how to read and understand an abstract
- to practice identifying keywords after your abstract

10.1 Overview

The abstract is by far the shortest section of a research paper, and hence it represents the shortest chapter in this textbook. The abstract section brings us full circle in the research paper writing process. Recall from 5.6.A the abstract of the article *The Influence of Herbs and Spices on Overall Liking of Reduced Fat Food.*

This was the first section that we read from this study, and we did so in order to understand the most essential aspects of this research project: the topic, the problem it is attempting to solve, the research question, the procedure, the outcome, and the implications. The abstract gave us all this information in a concise and straightforward manner, providing a window into the research study and perhaps enticing us to read further without using flowery or subjective language.

With hindsight, though, we can also see the direct relationship of *The Influence of Herbs and Spices* abstract with each of the individual sections of the research paper: the introduction, the methodology, the results, and the discussion/conclusion section. This is an important benefit of gaining experience with both reading and writing scientific research papers: when researching articles in the future, you will be able to understand abstract sections in an increasingly analytical manner and visualize how the entire paper will unfold.

10.2 Purpose

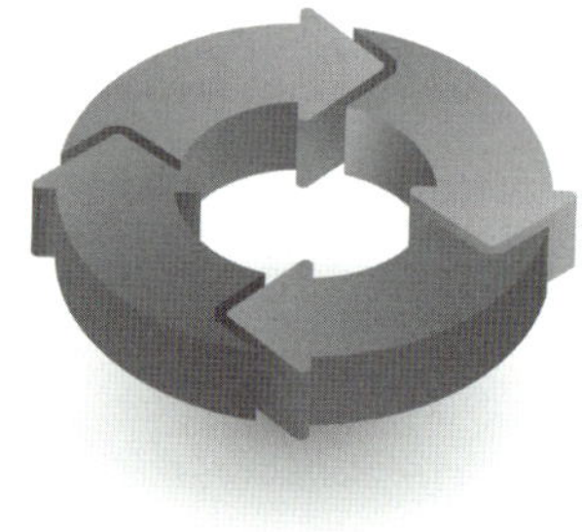

Not only does the abstract bring us full circle with the research paper, it also brings us full circle with this textbook, which began with the core elements of paragraph writing. Essentially, the abstract is a summary paragraph which represents the first contact any reader will have with your research paper. Without a well-written abstract, a research paper might fail to draw an audience and achieve any kind of recognition for its accomplishments.

All abstracts have three primary aims:

1. to clearly summarize your research paper by encapsulating the most important information from each section in it
2. to intrigue readers enough to continue reading your research paper
3. to connect your research project to specific topics or concepts (called keywords) so that your potential readers can find your article while searching for scientific papers which might provide insight into their own research

A final point to make about the abstract is that in order to write it in the right way, it needs to be the last phase in your writing process. Authors are often asked by publishing companies or conferences to provide an abstract well before a research paper has been completed, and thus must invert the writing process out of practical necessity. In these cases, though, it will eventually have to be revised; how could we possibly report the results, findings, and achievements of a research study when they do not yet exist? Ultimately, it is best to wait until the very end, when you truly have the advantage of hindsight and reflection.

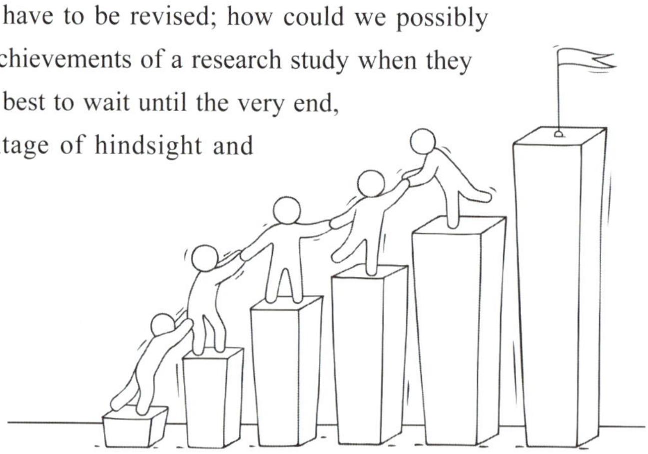

10.3 Language

The first language issue to consider with the abstract is to consider the appropriate verb tense for each section you are summarizing. The introduction section typically overviews general ideas, recent research, and key points about your study such as the initial hypothesis; hence, the *simple present*, *present perfect*, and *simple past* tenses might be used. On the other hand, the summaries of the methodology and results sections should mostly be written in the *simple past tense* as these sections describe actions that are completed. Finally, the overview of the discussion/conclusion section should focus on simple present or perhaps future tense, as this section is a reflection on what the findings of the study mean in general.

The second language issue to keep in mind is that after writing your abstract, you will need to select several *keywords* – somewhere between 3 and 4 should be sufficient – which relate to the most essential and relevant topics of your research study. These keywords will be placed at the bottom of the abstract, and they are very important because readers tend to search by keywords when they are looking for research in their field.

A final language issue to note about the abstract is that it is the information itself that needs to take precedence. While it is true that the abstract is essentially a paragraph, you do not need to think of this paragraph in the same manner that you did in the first four chapters of this book. For example, many abstracts do not contain clear transitions from one sentence to the next, nor do they follow the typical paragraph structure. You do not need to organize your abstract with a topic sentence, supporting sentences, and a concluding sentence. Instead, think of the abstract as distilling the most relevant information and findings in your research project. The style of an abstract should ultimately be economical and straightforward. The reason for this relates to the aims of your potential readers, who are primarily trying to determine if your research paper is useful and relevant for them.

10.4 Goals and Structure

To expand upon the main ideas from 10.3, your goals for this section are to summarize a number of *key points* from your research paper, which will be outlined below. The structure of the abstract does not need to follow the 'opening/body/closure' structure from the previous research chapters in this book. Instead, your primary aim is to select key information from the introduction, methodology, results, and discussion/conclusion section. Between two and three sentences for each research section should be sufficient, meaning your abstract will comprise roughly eight to ten sentences in total. To help you consider what information to select, you can use the following model:

❖ Key points from the introduction section

When abstracting information from your introduction section, consider the following ideas:

- the most relevant background information in your study
- the purpose of your study
- the problem that your study is addressing
- a general explanation of your research paper

❖ Key points from the methodology section

When abstracting information from your methodology section, consider the following ideas:

- the key procedures involved in your research study
- the key materials that were used in your research study

❖ Key points from your results section

When abstracting information from your results section, consider the following ideas:

- the key data outcomes of your study
- the decision about your original hypothesis
- possible implications of the data outcomes of your study

❖ Key points from your discussion/conclusion section

When abstracting information from your discussion/conclusion section, consider the following ideas:

- the main achievement(s) of your study
- the strengths and weaknesses of your study
- suggestions for future work and improvements related to your study

Read the abstract below:

The Relationship Between Paper's Absorption Ability and a Liquid's Viscosity

Abstract

The capillary action between a liquid and the surface of a solid allows the liquid to absorb through small holes of the absorbing material. In this case, the viscosity made by symmetric degree of the molecular structure of the liquid interrupts the absorption of the liquid to absorb through the solid's small holes. The purpose of this study was to find out how the ability of the absorption would change according to the liquid's viscosity. The absorbing ability of the paper pulp in the case of using three liquids having different viscosities – water, ethanol, and olive oil – was measured by comparing the differences between the initial wetted length (3 cm) of the paper by a liquid in the beaker and the wetted length after 60 seconds so that the vertically standing paper pulp absorbed some amount of the liquid. This measurement showed that a liquid which has large viscosity interrupts the absorbing liquid of the paper pulp more strongly. Furthermore, if there was only a small difference in viscosity between liquids, it could also produce a significant difference in the absorption ability. This indicates that when the liquid absorbed through the pipe due to the capillary action between the liquid and paper's wall, the degree of symmetry affects the value of viscosity to resist the capillary action. Further research studies are still needed to test a greater range of liquids and types of paper to enhance the findings of the current study.

Keywords : Capillary Action, Liquid Viscosity, Absorption

10.4.A

Discuss the following questions about the above abstract with your partner(s).

1. Relate each sentence in this abstract to a specific point in the model provided in 10.4.
2. State the verb tense in each sentence and why it is used.
3. Explain why the three keywords from the abstract have been selected. Are there any other keywords that the author might have considered?

10.5 Reading

Recall from previous chapters the research paper entitled *The Insulation Performance of Bubble Wrap Attached to Windows*. Read the paper in its entirety, then proceed to 10.6.

The Insulation Performance of Bubble Wrap Attached to Windows

Introduction

Due to poor window insulation, a great deal of energy has been wasted in indoor heating during the winter. According to the Korea Electric Power Corporation (2017), the electricity usage of Korea has increased 0.5% every year, and winter is one of the peak periods of annual electricity usage. Overuse of energy for heating carries not only a substantial cost, but also damages the environment by burning an increasing amount of fossil fuel. A heated room can maintain its temperature using a small amount of energy if it is well insulated. The most common areas of a house where heat leaks occur are glass windows, window frames, and door frames; therefore, these areas need to be examined to improve insulation efficiency. An insulation sheet, which is a heat retention material used to insulate rooms, can be easily attached to windows to effectively retain heat. This sheet works similarly as a double window – a window with two layers of glass – by forming a layer of air. Originally, bubble wrap was designed to protect fragile objects from being transported, but it has also been proven to work as an effective insulation method.

General methods currently used for indoor insulation include applying Styrofoam to the frames of windows and doors, constructing a double window to create a layer of air between the windows, and installing an air curtain where doors open frequently to stop heat from escaping. Bubble wrap is believed to be the most economical and effective solution, as demonstrated by Lee (2017) in a study that proved bubble wrap attached to windows can increase the room temperature by 2-3 degrees Celsius. The benefits of bubble wrap has lead many people to use it as an insulator today. In spite of this, there have been very few academic studies to examine its efficacy. Although several characteristics of bubble wrap were researched by existing studies, there has been no research about the effect of multilayer cases (**Bae, Kang, Choi, & Choi, 2017**).

The aim of this study was to find the optimal number of layers which maximizes the performance of bubble wrap insulation. The hypothesis of this experiment was that as the number of bubble wrap layers increases, the performance of the insulation would increase as well. This paper will demonstrate the performance of insulation in correlation with the number of layers of bubble wrap. The results from this study can be applied to real life by helping people use bubble wrap more effectively and reducing the amount of energy used for heating.

Methodology

This study was performed in November 2018 in an indoor environment. The purpose of the test was to determine the insulation effect of bubble wrap attached to a window. A crucial variable of the experiment was the terminal temperature (also called equilibrium temperature), which is the temperature of an object when the thermal conduction is in a steady state condition. By measuring the terminal temperature of the constant-powered object, the thermal conductivity of the object, which represents how well a given material delivers heat, can be found via a relatively straightforward equation. **Zhang, Jun, and Rhee (2016)** proposed that the standard method of measuring indoor insulation effect should measure both thermal conductivity and light transmittance, a term related to sunlight exposure. Due to a lack of equipment, however, only thermal conductivity was measured in this experiment.

A 40 cm sized cubic box made with Styrofoam boards was considered a model for a house. One of the side faces of the box was opened and used as a position of the window, and an acrylic board with 0.5 cm thickness was used as the window. Based on the assumption that heat only escapes at the window, Styrofoam (a strong insulation material) was used. A 220V-30W light bulb was installed in order to apply heat, and a temperature sensor was placed in the box at a distance of 15 cm to avoid any direct effect from the bulb. Bubble wrap with a bubble radius of 0.5 cm was then attached to the window and installed to face the inside of the box. The size and thickness of all bubble wrap sheets were kept constant, and the numbers of layers varied from one to five. A bare acrylic board without bubble wrap served as the control group for this test.

The experiment was conducted as follows: First, the air in the box was ventilated, and the room temperature was then measured. Next, the window with bubble wrap attached to it was carefully taped on the opened side of the box. After the box was ready, the light bulb was turned on. From this point onwards, the temperature of the box was checked consistently to see when the box reached its terminal temperature. Once the box temperature stabilized, it meant that it had reached its terminal temperature. In this experiment, the box reached its terminal temperature after approximately 50 minutes. Finally, the terminal temperature was recorded. The control group and layer groups (from one to five) were then tested, and the terminal temperature measurement was repeated seven times in three-minute intervals.

Reaching the terminal temperature meant that the power of the light bulb and thermal energy loss rate of the box were the same. To prevent heat from escaping, the holes in the bulb wire and sensor wire were sealed tightly. The thermal conductivities of the various layers of bubble wrap were then calculated.

Results

The insulation efficiency of bubble wrap was estimated by measuring the temperature differences (ΔT) between the inside and outside of the Styrofoam cubic box; this determined the optimal number of bubble wrap layers. Fig. 1 indicates that temperature differences between the inside and the outside of the cubic box increased as the number of bubble wrap layers increased. The largest temperature difference (14.7 °C) was recorded when the cubic box was covered with five layers of the bubble wrap, while the smallest (12.3 °C) was measured when there was no bubble wrap.

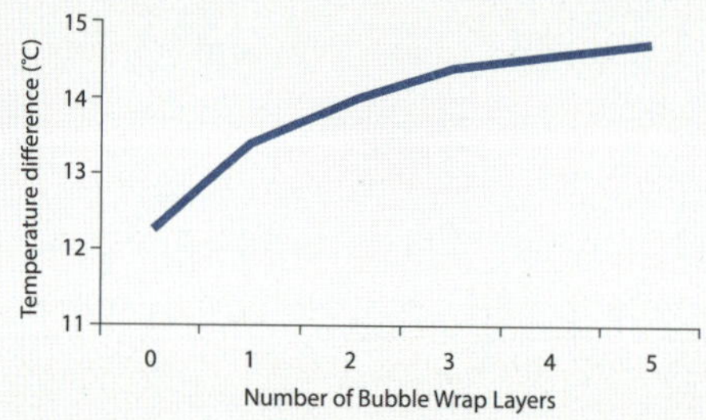

Figure 1. Temperature differences between the inside and the outside of the Styrofoam cubic box (ΔT, ℃) depending on the number of bubble wrap layers.

The slopes of temperature differences ($\Delta T_n - \Delta T_{n-1}$) were then calculated in order to estimate the optimal number of bubble wrap layers as reported in Table 1. As can be seen, the slope change of the temperature differences between the inside and the outside of the cubic box was the largest (1.13 °C) when the cubic box was wrapped with one layer of the bubble wrap; however, it was the smallest (0.14 °C) when the bubble wrap layers increased from four to five. The slopes of the temperature difference changed substantially as the number of bubble wrap layers increased to three. As the layers increased to four and then five, the slope changes gradually decreased.

Table 1. The slopes of the temperature difference depending on the number of bubble wrap layers.

Layer Increment	0 → 1	1 → 2	2 → 3	3 → 4	4 → 5
$\Delta T_n - \Delta T_{n-1}$ (℃)	1.13	0.60	0.43	0.19	0.14

Discussion/Conclusion

Prior research has documented the effect of qualitative factors of bubble wrap such as air tightness (**Bae et al., 2017**) and type (Seo, 2015) in improving insulation efficiency. However, these studies have either been purely theoretical or have focused on specialized bubble wrap which is not available to normal consumers. This study was done to investigate questions about multilayered bubble wrap and give practical advice to consumers; hence, it has a different focus from the aforementioned studies. Previous experiments have indicated that the insulation performance improved as the number of layers increased, but the improvement progressively decreased with the number of layers. Ultimately, statistical inference tests demonstrated that there was a significant improvement up to the third layer, but not beyond it. The negligible improvement that was found in four or more layers must be due to the economic principle of diminishing returns.

However, the results of this study do not necessarily suggest that everyone should attach three layers of bubble wrap to their window. One layer of insulation might be sufficient in some cases (such as one's economic circumstances) and, if so, it is not recommended to add more. Adding a second or third layer of insulated bubble wrap still saves energy efficiently, but beyond that the economic efficiency declines. Two sheets of bubble wrap cost twice as much as one, but the insulation efficiency improves at a much smaller rate.

This study had a number of strengths. The first major advantage was that due to the simplicity in the test's design, analyzing the results was a very straightforward process which almost entirely involved examining the temperature difference, or ΔT. The result ΔT is easily understood and interpreted; furthermore, it has a clear relationship with basic scientific theories from thermodynamics and other fields. Another notable benefit is that the results obtained from the study can be easily applied in real life. However, some limitations are worth noting. The most significant drawback was that this study did not consider light transmittance in relation to insulation performance. Both thermal conductivity and light transmittance should be considered when measuring the insulation performance of a window attached insulation sheet as **Zhang et al. (2016)** proposed. The ideal insulator is one with low thermal conductivity and high light transmittance. However, only the thermal conductivity was tested in this study due to a lack of equipment. In adding an extra layer, the conductivity increases and transmittance decreases; thus, it has an inverse effect. For this reason, the results from the current experiment may have overestimated the insulation performance. Future studies which include the light transmittance are needed to ensure greater accuracy. The next issue is that this study only used one type of bubble wrap. Different results may occur with different kinds of bubble wrap. For this experiment, the formula would have to be newly constructed in a different form since the thickness L of each bubble wrap varies, and ΔT could not be used. Future studies should therefore include a more diverse range of bubble wrap types.

References

Bae, M.J., Kang, J.S., Choi, K.S., & Choi, H.J. (2017). The effect of the attached glazing and windbreak on the thermal performance and air tightness of sliding windows. *KIEAE Journal, 17*(4), 59-65. http://doi.org/10.12813/kieae.2017.17.4.059

Korea Electric Power Corporation. (2017). Statistics of electric power in Korea. *Korea Electric Power Corporation Statistic Report, 86.*

Lee, K.M. (2017). Overuse boiler 'stupid', insulation bubble wrap 'great'. *Bulgyo News*. 2017.12.15. Retrieved from http://www.ibulgyo.com/news/article62633

Seo, J.G. (2015). Evaluation of insulation efficiency of windows and doors according to insulation sheet (bubble wrap) type and location. *Facilities Journal, 44*(11), 72-74.

Zhang, X., Jun, G., & Rhee, K.M. (2016). Comparative evaluation of thermal insulation and solar heat gain in bubble wrap attached window. *Journal of Architectural Institute of Korea, 36*(2), 565-566.

A Final Note on Citations

The first time you mention multiple authors (three or more) in APA, you need to list all of them in the text of your paper by their last names. If you refer to them later in your paper then you should use first author only in addition to – 'et al.'. When you use 'et al.' you need to place a period after the al. as this is a Latin abbreviation of the expression *et alia*, which means 'and others'.

The use of 'et al.' applies to three authors or more. In the case of two authors, they should always be named throughout the paper.

In the student sample paper in 10.5, note the following (they have been highlighted for ease of reference):

Example:

… (Bae, Kang, Choi, & Choi, 2017) … later in the paper becomes … (Bae et al., 2017) …

Example:

... Zhang, Jun, and Rhee (2016) ... later in the paper becomes ... Zhang et al. (2016)

If two authors or multiple authors are named within the text then 'and' should be used before the last author in the list, but if the names are within the parentheses the ampersand (&) can be used instead:

Example:

Compare: ... Zhang, Jun, and Rhee (2016) ... with ... (Zhang, Jun, & Rhee, 2016)

Note: In the abstract, you should note that the paragraph indentation is different from the paragraphs in each section of your research paper, in that, the abstract is not indented.

Compare the following:

Abstract
The capillary action between a liquid and a surface of solid allows the liquid to absorb |

Introduction
⟶ Due to the poor insulation of windows, a great deal of energy has been wasted in

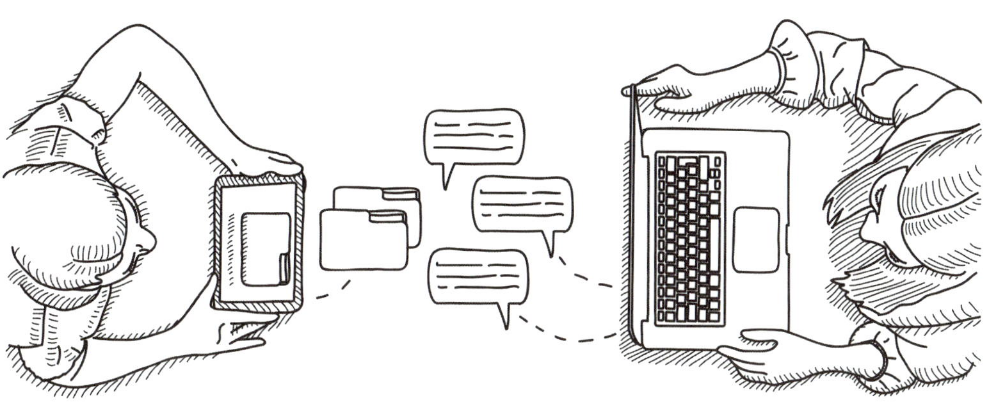

10.6 Writing

10.6.A

Using the model from 10.4 and information from the research paper in 10.5, write an abstract for *The Insulation Performance of Bubble Wrap Attached to Windows* in the space below.

Abstract

10.6.B

Compare and contrast your abstract with a partner's. Which information in your abstract is the same, and which is different? Are you both following the model from 10.4?

10.6.C

After reviewing your abstracts, write 3 keywords which you think represent the most important topics of this research project.

Keywords: ______________________

10.6.D

Read the abstract for the research paper *The Insulation Performance of Bubble Wrap Attached to Windows* and compare both your abstract and the keywords you selected with the sample.

The Insulation Performance of Bubble Wrap Attached to Windows

Abstract

As house insulation is an important issue in the winter, many people use bubble wrap as a window insulator which is convenient and inexpensive to install. In this study, the optimal number of bubble wrap layers attached to a window was investigated in order to provide real-life advice on maximizing the insulation efficiency of bubble wrap. More specifically, the experiment was conducted to measure the thermal conductivity of bubble wrap attached to a window. The window was placed on a face of a cubic Styrofoam box, and a light bulb was turned on inside of the box to apply constant heat. The terminal temperature difference of the inside and the outside of the box was measured. Although the terminal temperature rose every time by adding each layer, the magnitude of variation became smaller. The statistical analysis showed that there was no significant difference after three layers. The equation $\Delta T_n - \Delta T_{n-1}$ was used for statistical analysis, which has a direct mathematic relationship with thermal conductivity. The outcome of the experiment reveals that three is an optimal number of bubble wrap layers; in other words, a layer after the third does not provide any remarkable improvement on insulation performance. Since this study did not consider light transmittance, further studies are needed to make a comprehensive conclusion.

Keywords : Insulation, Bubble Wrap, Terminal Temperature

Writing Your Abstract

- This is the end of Chapter 10. It is now time for you to think about the abstract which you will write to summarize your research paper.
- You should first consider the key information from each section in your research paper that you want to report in your abstract.
- You should next consider the most appropriate verb tense for each section
- After that, you should select 3 or 4 keywords which represent the most important topics in your research study.
- After you have created your rough draft, use the revision checklist below to make editorial changes.

Revision Checklist

Did you ...

☐ follow the model as outlined in 10.4?

☐ convey the information in your study in a concise but effective manner?

☐ select keywords that will increase the readership of your research paper?

☐ think about the key points to include from the four sections of your research paper?

☐ format your abstract paragraph without an indentation?